#Blessed

#Blessed

*Intentional Gratitude in a World that
Celebrates Self Everything*

Laura A. Pyne

#Blessed: Intentional Gratitude in a World that Celebrates Self Everything

© 2021 Laura A. Pyne

A publication of Take Two Publishing in Harrisburg, Pennsylvania

Cover design: Laura A. Pyne
Interior design: Benjamin Vrbicek

Paperback ISBN: 978-0-578-90521-1

For my kids: may you live authentic lives full of God's abundant blessings, whether they fit the definition you see in the culture you're immersed in or not.

Contents

Introduction

Blessed.

I know what you're thinking: *"How overdone."*

All you have to do is sign into social media to be quickly overwhelmed by humblebrags disguised as "#blessed's."

You—and I—are also surrounded by messages that scream "self."

Self-empowerment. Self-achievement. Self-worth. The photos, the smiles, the lavish travel, they're all less-obvious examples of worldly happiness, the "I deserve more" mentality, and more.

We know this, yet, we find ourselves wanting. I know I do.

Even popular voices in and out of the Christian world promote these examples of what we are supposed to aspire to. Yet, every time we encounter these messages, these brags, these Photoshopped examples of "perfection," something is missing: gratitude for where we are, who we are, and *who we belong to.*

Maybe it's assumed. But, maybe—more often than not—it's just forgotten. We, as a culture, have become so focused on chasing what the world considers "#blessed," that we don't even know what real gratitude, intentional gratitude, looks and feels like.

It's time to change that. It's time to put gratitude—whether we feel it or not—first. It's time to be grateful *before* we chase our aspirations and desires. It's time to be intentional.

Recent times have brought new needs and issues to the forefront. From wildfires and chaos in different areas of the world, to a global pandemic, to eye-opening, heart-shaking examples of racial injustice here in the United States, feeling like we're standing on solid ground, let alone experiencing real gratitude and the peace it brings, has become a constant struggle for many of us.

I don't know where you're at today. I don't know where our world happens to be today or what new struggles we're facing as a global society. I don't know if you're in a place of struggle or if things are going great or if you're somewhere in the middle. But, I do know this: there is room for gratitude—Christ-centered gratitude—in your life.

I'd like to challenge you to chase it in this world of ours that screams "self" everything. When gratitude comes first, it's hard to get stuck in the negatives, in the comparisons and in the places where *we* come first.

Let's take it back. Let's start a movement where heart-deep gratitude comes first, just like it always should have. Are you in?

Special Note Before Going Forward

I started writing this book a long time ago . . . in 2018 to be exact. And for some reason, time and time again, I'd set it aside. I never understood, I felt as though God was calling me to share about gratitude, but then couldn't find the words to write. For me, this is usually a signal that I need to wait.

For someone who is also a planner who wants to continually move forward, this is often a frustrating place to find myself. But generally, I've learned that it means I've got to slow down and learn a lesson or two before going any further.

What I didn't realize was that in this time of waiting, our whole world was about to be shaken up.

I'm not sure what the future holds, but as this book is being written, here in the United States we are still fully immersed in the new world that has come about as a result of COVID-19. Life is opening back up, but it all feels a little unsteady. To be super honest, the laundry pile I mention at the beginning of chapter one (I promise, this will make sense soon!) has never felt farther away.

While that pile is still the beginning of my own gratitude

journey, and a real marker of change in my life and my relationship with God, so much has changed.

Experiencing 12+ months of quarantine, socially-distanced friendships, hardships, job losses, fear of the future, and a new type of isolation has changed a lot of hearts. A lot of us are still wondering what it all means for the future. We don't know what the world will look like after the coronavirus goes away, or if it will ever really be "gone." Some of us are still reeling from varying opinions and attitudes that became prevalent during the whirlwind. As businesses begin to reopen, masks start to come off, and the world starts to resume in this "new normal," we're face to face with things in a way we never were before.

We've all had a lot of time to focus on the world through a different lens. While there have been positives to spending more time with family, it's also been a time that feels like a magnifying glass has been held over the tiny cracks in our lives and in our hearts, bringing a lot of pain out in the open along with many emotions we've never had to deal with before.

Personally, it's made gratitude something that has required even more intentionality than usual. As I worked through the words in this book, I had to check my heart time and time again. It has been hard. It has been frustrating. And yet . . . every time I've started my day with gratitude, God has shown himself in new, great ways, restoring hope and fixing broken pieces of my heart.

This matters. It matters because during this time, I—

and all of us—have seen a lot more of what others have to share on social media. We've gained a new level of resentment for those who seem to just float through this whole thing unscathed. We've been forced to deal with "what if's" about our financial futures that we never thought we'd face. We've watched people hoard goods in a way that makes it hard to put others first. We've witnessed despair at levels that are hard to understand. We've seen the hurt of our Black friends who've faced generational injustice that we can't imagine—or simply didn't want to—just a few months ago, and we've tried to find a way to move forward, to become bridge builders who stand for those who need us, to become a voice for those who are hurting.

Honestly, in all of it, gratitude has probably been something we haven't had a lot of time to focus on. Maybe that's where you find yourself today—no matter what today looks like for you—or where the world has come since the low point that was the start of 2020.

Maybe your heart feels like mine many times . . . farther away from gratitude than it ever has before.

Maybe that's the point. Maybe now is the time that we need to get intentional in a way we just never have had to before. Perhaps right now is the best time to shift from gratitude as a positive emotion, to gratitude as something that's a choice, a choice that changes hearts and brings people together, spreading the love of God like—maybe—few other things ever could. Maybe now, today, the new ground zero, is the best place to start.

Let's build together. Let's establish the best possible foundation for moving forward. Let's do this . . . k?

Heart Check Before We Start

1. What does "gratitude" mean to you, today, where you are right now? How would you define it?

2. In what ways do you feel like you just don't measure up? What are you using as your measuring stick, or, to what are you comparing yourself?

3. What are you hoping to learn—or gain—from this book as you move forward?

Gratitude Is a Choice

"I cannot do another load of laundry," I thought. "I cannot. I will not. Who needs clean clothes anyway?"

I was standing in my laundry room in the home my husband and I shared with our four kids—three boys, aged 5, 3 and 2 months, and one little girl, also 2 months, a twin to our youngest boy—in Asheville, North Carolina, doing *another* load of laundry. At this point, we averaged 1–2 loads a day. Baby clothes are not for the faint of heart!

I had work projects to focus on, client emails that I felt so far behind on. My body was still recovering from a challenging delivery that the twins and I were lucky to have come out of alive. Winter was setting in and most of all, I. Was. Tired. Baby wake times were challenging; twins felt impossible about 99% of the time and there was no end in sight. I'm not a crier. But, during this time, I felt as though tears were falling down my face more often than they weren't.

"Overwhelmed" felt like a constant description of my mental state.

I felt stuck and couldn't see the blessings that were literally surrounding me. It had been a frequent theme for my worldview at the time. I couldn't see anything but mountains in front of me most of the time.

Only this time, something flickered inside me. "Be grateful."

For laundry? No thanks.

"Be grateful for the laundry."

I heard the thought loud and clear. I stopped folding and thought about it. When I did, I couldn't think of anything else.

This laundry? It meant I had a family of little ones depending on me, little ones that some others would do almost anything to be folding laundry for. I was in a comfortable house in a dreamy location in the western North Carolina mountains. Everyone was healthy. The laundry was a reflection of blessings that were far more than I deserved or had taken the time to consider.

Thank you for this laundry, I prayed. *And, for everything it means.*

This example? It's pretty small when you think about the grander things in life. But, it was a turning point in my life that I've looked back on many times since. Between that day and today, our family has added yet another little one. We've moved from North Carolina to Pennsylvania to Virginia and back to Pennsylvania—a process that never seemed "easy." The laundry piles have gotten bigger, as have the stains that have accompanied them. Our kids' grass stains and boo-boos have become real fears, concerns, and uncertainties. Our professional lives have taken numerous twists and turns during which anxieties have taken root in unexpectedly deep ways.

But, still, I fold. And when I do, when I catch the begrudging feeling that often accompanies this chore that—for some reason—has always been my least favorite, I find myself saying a prayer of gratitude that seems to allow everything else to fall into place.

When I'm truly thankful for something, how can negativity take over? *I really don't think it can.*

When Grumbling Represents a Deeper Trouble

This choice? It represents a turning point in my life, a moment that smacked me in the face and reminded me how far I was running from the truth that not all journeys look the same. It reminded me that I was stuck in a phase that was all about me—my wants, my dreams, my plans.

I needed to course-correct, and I needed to do it fast.

I'm not alone in this. I don't think that "me" mentality is rare; in fact, I think our culture celebrates it more now than ever before.

As women, we're especially susceptible to it.

We are told every day in both direct, clear messages, and in more subtle ways, that we deserve it all. We deserve to chase *our* dreams and *our* happiness. We deserve to be wildly successful, living lives filled with Insta-worthy smiles, memories and moments. We deserve husbands who meet our every need, supporting all of those dreams and goals. We deserve comfort and ease. This world has become more accessible than ever before and it's *ours* for the taking.

It all sounds pretty wonderful, doesn't it?

But, when those lofty expectations aren't met (maybe even worse, when they seem to be met for everyone around us: *thanks social media*), we feel unsatisfied. We believe we deserve more. We feel as though our "needs" (which are more likely desires, but we'll get there) aren't met and we complain.

Whether our complaints lead to outward grumbling, inward dissatisfaction or a complete inability to see the blessings that surround us, they all represent the same thing: a deep-rooted soul problem reflecting our focus on ourselves, instead of the bigger mission our creator has called each and every one of us to.

Friends, we have been called to *BIG* things:

- To helping others (Hebrews 6:10)
- To serving others rather than indulging the flesh (Galatians 5:13)
- To serving the Lord faithfully (1 Samuel 12:24)
- To following the Lord (John 12:26)

- To being obedient to the Lord (Joshua 22:5)

And so much more.

When we become so nearsighted that we can only focus on our current dislikes and discomforts, how can we possibly be living out our bigger, truer callings?

How can we serve others or live lives that reflect the grace and love of our creator?

Simply: we can't.

We all have tasks that we dislike. We all have experiences we'd rather not focus on. But, when the grumbling starts to take hold, I think we're called to think about what it represents and to consider whether it might be a symptom of a bigger problem—a reliance on ourselves instead of God, and a focus on our own desires that might be pushing us away from the mission he has placed us on. For me, this was certainly the case and I know *I'm not alone.*

You'll hear this alot in this book: while our journeys are all different, we share so much more—both good and bad—than we often recognize.

But, deeper issues aside, there is good news here for believers: we have hope!

Gratitude Starts with a Choice

The Bible tells us time and time again to "give thanks" and "praise the Lord." The jury is out on exactly *how many* times this is commanded, but, let's all agree that it is *a lot.*

My favorite example comes in 1 Thessalonians 5:18

which reads: *"Give thanks in all circumstances; for this is the will of God in Christ Jesus for you."*

It doesn't say "give thanks, except when you're uncomfortable." It doesn't tell us to give thanks when we feel like our pictures appropriately conform to the hashtag-worthy examples of worldly "goodness" that we're surrounded by.

It tells us to give thanks in *all* circumstances. Every. Single. One. It also tells us that this is God's will for us; for *all* of us, whether we live in mansions and drive new cars or wonder where we'll find the cash to put dinner on the table or make rent this month. There's no qualifier, there's no exception, there's just a command.

This doesn't mean muttering a simple prayer of thanks every time we see a blessing around us—though, this might be a simple enough first step that gets our hearts moving in the right direction.

This form of thanks is a way that we can praise our Lord today while looking forward to the blessings he has for us in the life to come. When we make the effort to be grateful in *all* circumstances, as we are commanded, our lives become so filled with gratitude that is out of this world, that it overflows from every part of our beings.

This kind of gratitude is both heart-changing and life-changing. It reflects beyond our circumstances and our own lives out to those around us, pointing them back to the one who loves them more than they may even be able to fathom, let alone believe, right now in their own circumstances.

This kind of out-of-this-world praise rooted in deep-reaching, all-encompassing gratitude doesn't come naturally; in fact, the opposite is probably true. But, it is a choice we can make every day, a choice with life-changing, life-altering, life-improving ramifications!

Research Backs It Up

Here's the thing: gratitude is not reserved for followers of Christ alone, though, it may look different for those of us who are believers. We have someone to be grateful to, and a hope to grasp that others—until they place God at the center of their lives—simply cannot.

But, this knowledge aside, even the world believes in gratitude. An article published in UC Berkeley's *Greater Good Magazine* touted research that—in 2017—confirmed measurable health benefits of living lives that reflect gratitude. Of the 300 study participants described in the piece, those that took specific steps to practice gratitude experienced fewer negative emotions, less depression, and less anxiety.[1]

Even more notable, MRIs of the brains of those participating in the study found that those taking specific steps toward gratitude (writing letters of gratitude to others in this particular instance) had brains that looked different! They had more neural sensitivity in their medial prefrontal cortexes—the area of the brain associated with a greater

---

[1] Brown, Joshua, and Joel Wong. "How Gratitude Changes You and Your Brain." *Greater Good Magazine.* Berkeley, 6 June 2017. Web. 11 Nov. 2020.

ability to learn and make decisions.

Gratitude *rewires our brains* in the best way possible.

According to the study, "Gratitude reverses our priorities to help us appreciate the people and things we do."

Greater appreciation? Better priorities? Think of the implications if this became the norm for more of us and those around us.

Gratitude Takes Time

We're commanded to be grateful in all situations. Scientific research backs up the tangible health benefits of practicing gratitude. So . . . why is it so hard?

The answer is two-fold: it's not "natural," and it takes time.

We live in a society that places so much attention on changing our attitudes to accomplish our dreams and on the importance of chasing the things we want that influencers all around us tell us "we deserve," that it's hard to feel anything other than "less-than."

Our houses are a disaster after a day of kids playing hard, but, that celebrity with 4 kids manages to keep her house looking like a magazine spread around the clock.

We don't measure up.

That writer who says the same things we do makes the *New York Times* bestsellers list, but no one reads our blogs.

We don't measure up.

Our resumes say all the right things, but we can't get a return call, let alone an interview. Meanwhile, our best friend has turned down 3 opportunities this week that we would have killed for.

We don't measure up.

Our fitness influencer friend not only has rock-hard abs, but makes a killing selling her products online, yet, we can't take off the baby weight and don't have time to even venture to the gym, nevermind spending hours a day chasing the ideal physique.

We don't measure up.

When we focus on how our real lives look, especially in comparison to that trendy, #blessed theme that seems to haunt our social feeds, we don't measure up: we can't. Even with the best filters and take after take to capture our best smiles and our most clutter-free angles, we cannot stay ahead or even keep up.

We aren't supposed to.

We are told that this life and this world will be hard; it will give us trouble (John 16:33). But, our God has overcome this world. We are told we will stand out. We are told our lives will look different. Sometimes this may feel like we simply can't make the mark (make no mistake, I am not confusing this sort of "not measuring up" with an excuse to practice laziness or to forget about finding ways to improve!), but maybe, just maybe, it means that it's time to make a different choice: the choice to be grateful.

According to the aforementioned study, personal experience and the experiences of others who have shared this focus-shift, intentional gratitude takes time: 12 weeks according to research.That's roughly 3 months.

For my own life, that meant 3 consecutive months of drudging through things that were hard and opting to give thanks anyway.

While that lightbulb moment in the laundry room was certainly a turning point, it didn't immediately change my heart. Heart change takes time, surrender, and a focus on biblical truth.

We, as a culture, aren't great with things that take time. We aren't wired to be patient. We're wired for instant answers, real-time communication, and results.

As I worked through this chapter, I watched the 2020 election unfold with the initial vote counting taking several days. It felt like an eternity. I watched friends cling to "diet" plans that promised instant change. I watched the world push to reopen immediately knowing full well that we were on the verge of a major surge, instead of waiting on a solution to the coronavirus situation that very few experts agreed on how to combat. I watched it become a political divide, and even a denominational divide as everyone picked sides and time dragged on and on.

It's funny though (maybe not funny in a literal way, but, stick with me), it seems that while we always default to "instant" or easy, those options rarely pan out. Have you noticed that trend?

When we rush, we make mistakes. We quit. We see less-than-stellar results. We get overwhelmed and find ourselves back in the place of not measuring up that we just talked about leaving. That's what makes gratitude so hard.

It's not fast. It's not easy. It sometimes opposes the very notion of everything we want to cling to. It requires a focus and dependence on something much bigger than ourselves. It's easier to focus on the ways we fall short and stay in that place, limited forever as far as the impact we can make in this world because our focus stays on ourselves. What a waste!

We owe it to ourselves, our world, and our God to get this right. Let's keep that in mind.

Before diving any further in this book, I want to be sure to reiterate and establish two things:

1. *Gratitude is a choice.* It starts with an effort to remember our place and our mission in this world, and to decide, regardless of our circumstances to focus on giving thanks and being grateful. No. Matter. What.

2. *Gratitude takes time.* Saying thank you today? It matters. But, it won't change everything, not on a big scale, not right away. You'll still feel the "I don't measure up" blues creep in. You'll still ask a lot of "why's" and feel many "less-than" moments, especially in the beginning. But, by making it a priority in your life, praying for assistance in the endeavor and committing to the long term, *it will change everything.*

Got it? Great! Let's keep moving forward!

Questions to Consider

1. In what areas of life do you feel "stuck" today?

2. What small steps could you take to practice thankfulness?

3. What practices and behaviors make you feel "less than?" Can you walk away from them?

4. In what ways has God blessed you that perhaps you haven't seen as a blessing before?

5. What are you anxious about today? How could you insert gratitude into that situation? What do you think the outcome could be?

Gratitude

As Intended and Commanded

Intentional gratitude.

To be honest, when I experienced my own radical "conversion" to living a life of gratitude, I didn't have a name for it. I realized that my life became more reliant upon God—and more joyful—when I focused on the things I had to be grateful for, rather than the things I wanted.

I thought I was onto something.

But then, I found it somewhere else—kind of. I'll explain the "kind of" in a bit.

The short of it, is that what felt so revolutionary, so freeing, to me, was actually pretty popular in the world surrounding me among people of all walks of life. At first, I thought it was great. Remember, even science touts the benefits of intentional gratitude. But soon . . . some differences started to set in, becoming more and more apparent rather quickly.

You see, I found a professing Christian who was quickly rising in both the secular and Christian worlds. She'd written a book that had taken off and her social media was filled with helpful tips for moms, business women, wives, and beyond. Friends from all walks of life became hooked on the message she had to share. I found many of her posts to be helpful and even considered attending a few events she'd be speaking at. After all, the message felt good!

Part of it—a large part of it—centered around gratitude, *intentional* gratitude.

I loved it. So, I dove in. But, the deeper I went, the more I dug in, and the more I tried to rationalize it all, what I found made me feel uneasy. I couldn't explain it then, but I can now.

I can say—and maybe you've experienced the same— that the "off-balance" sensation I felt wouldn't lift; it wouldn't go away. Something was just "off." When I get this feeling, it usually means it's time to dig deep, to jump into scripture, and to search for the right path, even if I can't put my finger on what is wrong.

You see, this version of "gratitude" I stumbled upon, had a more worldly slant: maybe that's why such a wide group of my friends and acquaintances were drawn to it. Who wouldn't be? (Let's be clear before moving forward, worldly doesn't mean "bad" in this situation, but it is extremely different from what we want to chase here).

While thankfulness was featured prominently (which is IMPORTANT and helpful for all of us!), it was also filled with both literal and figurative forms of "self." It taught those who paid attention to be grateful, but also to continue clawing forward toward their own hopes, dreams and plans. It had undertones that made it clear that, by working hard enough and prioritizing properly, you could achieve *anything*. Suddenly, gratitude had shifted into just another tool to help the practicer chase their own desires.

Do I believe in working hard to accomplish what matters to me? Of course! The Bible exhorts us to work hard!

But—and here's where it gets a little dangerous for those of us who profess to be followers of Christ—if those dreams aren't *bathed* in prayer, examined fully for motives and tested against scriptural truth, they could be the very things leading us away from our Creator, instead of toward his plans.

We'll dive deeper into this idea of chasing dreams later on, but for now, let's just stick with the fact that we need to practice caution in how we proceed during this undertaking. It's really easy to end up in the wrong spot and with the wrong intentions.

Sure, gratitude matters: but the intention behind it *and* the realization that it is what we are commanded to do, rather than a means to an end, are also critical.

If it's simply a springboard toward achieving what we want, our hearts aren't in the right spot. This is something we each need to check from time to time. Our motivations matter.

It Wasn't the Last Time

I share that story not to make a particular influencer look bad, or to question her heart; we, as humans, are not in the heart judging business. Thank goodness. I share to illustrate a common theme that has crept into our culture, one Christian influencer at a time.

This was not the only time I found this message underneath a pronunciation of gratitude. In fact, I started to notice it everywhere.

"Be thankful" the world screams at us from every direction, followed almost immediately by "*YOU* can achieve whatever *YOU* want . . . whatever *YOU* deserve."

As I started following these influencers, another pattern became common: those who shouted these messages seemed to fall hardest. Whether it was by walking away from the faith altogether, by beginning to believe and follow, then *lead* others into scriptural untruths, or something else, almost every time someone's "gratitude" message became tangled up in messages of "self," scripture began to lose its relevance. Followings increased, but truth decreased.

That's a scary thought. Yet, the trend surrounds us every single day.

Maybe It's Because Commandments Are Hard

On the outside, it might not feel like commandments are especially hard to follow. Not all of them at least. Don't kill? No problem. Don't steal? I'm also good with that.

But, what about others, even those that fall outside of the big 10? Don't covet (*How could we not? Who doesn't want nice things, especially the things that others make us feel like we need?*). Be a follower (*ouch*). Be grateful (*hmmm*).

I think this is where the conflict—and maybe the vortex we see Christian influencers, and ourselves, if we're honest, fall into every day—begins.

You see. When we believe in chasing dreams and doing "big" things, whatever they may be, we forget that God is in control and that his "big" dreams for our lives might feel pretty ordinary, maybe even really hard. When we settle on something like gratitude, it's really easy to let a little bit of "maybe if I'm grateful for this . . . I can achieve *that*" slip into our lives. We lose sight of the fact that our primary purpose in this world is to follow, not to lead.

I'm not talking about gender roles here. I'm not making a commentary on our roles as women. I believe God has given us strengths beyond what we can even imagine or identify as strengths. Instead, I'm talking about us as humans and believers.

Our primary role, maybe even our most basic commandment (outside of the great commandment of course—

Matthew 22—though, loving God is perhaps a prerequisite to following him) is to follow the Lord. Scriptures make it clear:

- You shall walk after the LORD your God and fear him and keep his commandments and obey his voice, and you shall serve him and hold fast to him. (Deuteronomy 13:4).
- And calling the crowd to him with his disciples, he said to them, "If anyone would come after me, let him deny himself and take up his cross and follow me." (Mark 8:34).
- Blessed is everyone who fears the LORD, who walks in his ways! (Psalm 128:1).
- For we are his workmanship, created in Christ Jesus for good works, which God prepared beforehand, that we should walk in them. (Ephesians 2:10).

The list goes on and on, but, you get the picture. To love God, and to serve him, we must become followers of his plans, his dreams and his story . . . not our own.

This is hard; I know it is for me. I *want* the bigger house. My Pinterest is filled with dream rooms with amazing views that often make up my dreams. I *want* kids who follow both my rules and God's. I *want* my business to grow and for people to notice my work. I *want* my husband to find success in his career, to travel the world and so on. I have no shortage of wants. I bet you have your own list. Maybe it's pretty similar to mine, maybe it's completely different.

But, unless those wants stem from God's purpose for my life, my following him wholeheartedly, and my denying myself, they do nothing but lead me away from what I'm here for.

For those of us who grew up in church, this "radical" calling often gets put on the back burner.

Many times this is because we don't have much of a "before" that demonstrates a miraculous "God did a miracle" conversion story to share. So, we let ourselves forget that God loving us and leading us is reason enough to shout it from the rooftops and overflow with gratitude.

To love Jesus, to call ourselves believers, whether we can remember a time before him in our lives or not, we are to follow him. We sing songs about it. We commit the verses to memory . . . but do we go all in?

Do we ask God to lead us? What if that request means he leads somewhere that doesn't fit into our five-year plan? How do we react if fellow believers or leaders lovingly tell us we might be off track? Do we react with grace? Do we take the necessary steps to follow, change, or repent?

It's easy to say we follow. It's easy to know with head-deep knowledge that it's what we are called to. But friends, the application is hard . . . so very life-changingly hard!

Gratitude in ALL Circumstances

This brings us back to the "gratitude" commandment we discussed in Chapter 1. We are commanded to live lives full of gratitude and praise. Only, instead of gratitude *just* when we feel as though it's deserved, or *only* when it's tied to good things, we are to reflect it *constantly*.

When our gratitude is tied to our own wants, or thankfulness for things that we feel as though we've achieved, or, material things that make no difference in the long run—though we should be happy for the blessings God has bestowed upon us, make no doubt about it—our intentionality is lost, tied up somehow in the chasing of our own plans, our own "self."

It can—and should—look different.

In college, my husband and I started at two different schools about an hour's drive apart. I made that drive more than anyone in either of our families (*hello gas money!*) would have liked to admit at the time. But, as I drove, I'd listen to the local Christian music station.

On one particular drive, popular Christian singer Jeremy Camp, who was just rising among the Christian music ranks, was on the air, sharing his testimony.

I didn't know at the time, but my then-boyfriend, now-husband, happened to be listening at the same time. The story would have lasting implications for our walks with Christ. For me, I'm talking about a pull the car over to have a tear-filled heart-to-heart with God implication that became a building block in my relationship with Christ. In fact the interview we heard served as a lightning strike for us both on our journeys back to God . . . But, that's a story for a different time.

What matters is this. For those of you who may not be familiar, Jeremy Camp lost his first wife to cancer, cancer that returned and was diagnosed right after they returned from their honeymoon. She praised God through it all, the ups and the downs, sharing that if her suffering brought one person to Jesus, it would all be worth it. The story has now been turned into a movie—*I Still Believe*. Maybe you've seen it. If you haven't, with a quick online search, you can find even more details . . . but the part that stuck with us both was what comes next.

In a CBN interview, Jeremy Camp is quoted as saying the following, similar to what he shared in the interview we both heard. He shared what happened in the immediate moment following her passing. I think his words sum it all up best:

> I was on my knees and I remember her sister saying, 'She is with Jesus now.' A grief fell over me that I can't describe. The weight of her suffering is over, but the grief is she's gone. We always had worship music playing in the background. I remember the Lord speaking into my heart and saying, 'Jeremy, I want you to stand up and worship me.' I remember standing up and raising my hands.[1]

Guys . . . think about this picture. Really think about it. This man lost the love of his life. At her deathbed, he

---

[1] Smith Haney, Audra. "Jeremy Camp: Melissa's Dying Wish." *CBN*. N.p. Web. 11 Nov. 2020.

feels God telling him to *worship*, not just to sing a song, but, to *worship*. He hears it and he does it, even though it's probably the last thing he *felt* like doing at the time.

Call it praise. Call it worship. Call it gratitude no matter the cost. Call it whatever you want: *THIS* is the kind of gratitude, the kind of life that we, as Christians are called to, gratitude that can *only* come from placing someone so much bigger than ourselves in the drivers seats of our lives, hanging on for the ride and being thankful no matter what comes.

This kind of gratitude looks different than standard thankfulness for things handed to us, or things we've achieved. Really, it is shocking, especially to an unbelieving world. It draws people to God in ways that our own meager efforts simply cannot. It is earth-shattering, life-changing and life-giving both for those of us who obey and those who watch it all play out. Better yet: it can't possibly come from a shallow or selfish place. It's a true reflection of Christ's place in our hearts and in our lives.

For some of us, this might feel more than a little off-putting. In fact, when I get into the nitty-gritty of it all with skeptical friends, it often all boils down to this (seeming) contradiction.

What about folks in concentration camps? Should they have been grateful? Torture victims? Those with devastating illnesses? Those who experience heart-wrenching loss like Jeremy Camp?

The radical answer here is *yes*.

Before you throw the book at the wall or in the trash, let's clarify. This isn't a "yes" that erases sadness or tears or heartbreak or suffering or sorrow. It's not "fake a smile and move on with life" sort of yes. But, rather, a yes that acknowledges our God is good and is on his throne and that a resolution for our pain and suffering might not be found on this side of heaven. This kind of gratitude can exist next to brokenness.

Gratitude in this place is hard and messy. And yet, it is vital.

It might be all we have left, a white-flag, a raised hand . . . and yet, God is there. When all else is stripped away, we learn he is enough. His grace is sufficient through, above, before, and after all life's circumstances.

This is the gratitude we are called to—not just a quick thank you when things are great and life is easy, but, an ability to trust in God's promise to fulfil his plans for our lives, not our plans for our life. This is gratitude when it's gritty, hard and the last thing we *want* on our own: gratitude as an outpouring of our following of Christ.

Sometimes getting to a place of gratitude like this requires getting on our knees in prayer and staying there for longer than we could imagine. It might require outside help and perspective, even (especially) professional help. It might take much longer than the simple 12–week formula we discussed in chapter one.

Nonetheless.

This is the kind of gratitude we are commanded to

practice. This is the kind of gratitude that God calls us to. It's hard. It requires getting intentional. Sometimes it's accompanied by the worst possible circumstances in our lives. And yet, it is heart-deep. It changes everything. And it's exactly what we *need*, all of us, whether we *want* it or not.

Isn't that a little different from what other voices in this world would have us hear? It's radical in the best possible way. What could this kind of gratitude mean for your heart? For your family? For your future? For your relationship with your creator?

Questions to Consider

1. How does gratitude bring us closer to God?

2. How does God's view of gratitude differ from what you see in the world surrounding you?

3. Why do you believe God commands us to be grateful and praise him, no matter what?

4. What hardships in your life have provided an opportunity to practice intentional gratitude? If you cannot think of any, write out what intentional gratitude might look like in your life moving forward.

Glass-Half-Empty Living Breeds Discontent

We've all found ourselves in "that" place at one point or another, the place where the hypothetical glass seems half empty even though we know it's full!

Maybe it's that trip to Disney World where one kid nearly broke a foot, another ended up in urgent care with a UTI, while two others came down with strep throat (no? Just me?).

Maybe it's the new job that we know God placed in our laps . . . but we can't seem to juggle it all and feel like we're failing at everything.

Maybe it's a new home or living situation that's more

than we can imagine, and yet, we can't stop focusing on all the work that comes with it, or, the features it doesn't have.

Maybe it's a spouse that loves us and our kids beyond words, yet, we can't stop focusing on what he *doesn't* do in a given day.

Maybe it's something else entirely. Maybe it's something new every day.

Whether you're able to recognize when you are stuck in the "glass half empty zone" yourself, or, whether you recognize it more in those around you, you're familiar with it. Often, we label certain people—maybe ourselves—more "negative" than others. But, here's the cold, hard truth.: we're not designed to be negative beings.

I'm not saying that we should walk around happy as unicorns and butterflies, without a care in the world (*hey "Trolls!"*), or that there's not a very real time and need to experience and work through grief. In fact, we just got into the raw truth of this in the last chapter. But, the daily negativity cycle we find ourselves—and others—stuck in? It's a symptom of discontent.

It also feels more prevalent today than ever before.

Why?

Simple: it's easier today to compare ourselves to others, even others we've never met or interacted with at all (and probably never will), who fall far beyond the realm of our own circle of friends and loved ones. In some ways, this is an enormous blessing. But, when it comes to overall contentment, it works against us.

Ads, Influencers, and Beyond

For me it usually starts with social media. "Smart" ads that start to know my online habits and conversations, displaying "relevant" ads have been a problem for me, in more ways than one.

A few years back, I found an online boutique that I fell in love with. The owner was (and is) a strong Christian who makes reasonably priced, modest clothes available. She had fun doing it. I was hooked (to be clear: I still am. I'm a huge fan of the business she's built and would encourage everyone I know to check them out. "Filly Flair" is the name of her incredible business if anyone needs some inspiration! And yet, I digress).

Because of my own personal leanings, it was quickly much more than this incredible boutique showing up in my social feed. ALL the clothes from ALL the companies started appearing, no matter where I turned online. Since my job involves me being active on social media, this became a problem.

Soon, I was purchasing whatever I felt like purchasing, whenever I felt like purchasing it. Not only that, I was comparing myself to the models on the screen. If a piece of clothing didn't fit me quite like it did them, I felt "less than." If I couldn't afford to buy *all* the things, I felt discontent. When my husband questioned where *another* box came from, I became defensive. The cycle turned something harmless and fun into something not so uplifting pretty quickly.

I found myself in conversations with friends who found themselves in the same spot as me. Online jokes went wild with it, memes filled with hiding where packages were coming from, companies offering slips that shared "congratulations, you've won!" to hide the fact that purchases were made at all, and races home to watch the mailman and hide packages became the norm.

Sure, there was humor, but, that humor also helped disguise an indicator of a deeper potential issue: discontent—especially when it leads to action—has real, lasting consequences.

For me, this went even deeper. See, I've struggled with body image issues since I was a teenager. I know (often on a head-deep level) that I was created by God, in his image. But, I also want to look a certain way. From destructive eating cycles to obsessive running and hours spent at the gym daily, I can go down a dark path quickly, and have. Clothes are often the beginning of this cycle; the patterns above only furthered the problem.

Left to my own devices, my online shopping habit could have had real negative implications (and in many cases, has). Financially. In my relationship with my husband. In my own persistent chasing of material things. In my relationship with Christ . . . the list could go on and on.

Luckily, ads are easy enough to turn off, and a husband who works in finance is hard to hide things from. There was a simple enough switch "off" for my own battle of discontent and needing "more." I was able to get back on track, enjoying—limited—purchases from what had become a business special to my heart. But, that's not always the case. Destructive habits that stem from these simple desires can be lasting, causing long-term damage.

We all have struggles. Yours may look different. Maybe you have yet to even admit that whatever you're struggling with may be coming between your relationship with God, your relationship with others, and your ability to practice gratitude. But, regardless of what it is, chances are, some level of discontent helps feed it. What you're facing might even feel like an impossible cycle with no end in sight.

It might feel impossible because rising above on your own strength *can* be impossible.

Staying above—even after the heart-conviction that causes change, can also be difficult, maybe even more difficult.

We all have struggles that we tend to fall into time and time again. Whether you call something like this a "pet" sin, or, would rather not acknowledge that you struggle with the same thing over and over again (though it's not new, and not unique, this has been the case throughout all of human history, referenced constantly and documented well in scripture!), the fact remains, getting ahead of these holds in our lives is hard. It takes effort, it takes intentionality, and—if we're honest—it takes God. Even 12–step programs include leaning into a higher power.

Humans weren't meant to fight alone!

What we're chasing after is often a reflection of our priorities . . . of what really matters most to us when everything else is stripped away.

We're Meant for More

By "more," I'm not talking about material things or experiences, though, that's exactly the message we're confronted with each and every day.

The *more* I'm talking about comes, once again, from the giver of life himself. For women struggling today with being the perfect mom, the Pinterest-worthy planner of all the parties, the employee that climbs the seniority ladder at work and beyond, that might just start with a 180–degree turn toward intentional gratitude and contentment.

Philippians 4:12–13 spells it out for us. You see, Paul wrote his letter to the Philippians at a time where he was in prison, very likely in Rome under the rule of Nero. I know you've heard of him. In fact, what you *have* heard probably doesn't even scratch the surface of how bad this time was for followers of Christ. From basic discrimination to all out persecution, crucifixions and burnings in the Colosseum, "bad" doesn't even scratch the surface of what members of the early church faced.

It's in this landscape that while encouraging the Philippians to seek salvation, Paul shared an important message, one that we can and should take to heart today. In the NIV version of the Bible, this passage reads:

I know what it is to be in need, and I know what it is to have plenty. I have learned the secret of being content in any and every situation, whether well fed or hungry, whether living in plenty or in want. I can do all things through him who gives me strength.

Most of us can recite the last part of that passage, many of us probably have songs in our heads from childhood that remind us we can do all things through him who gives us strength.

But, are we missing what comes right before that?

Paul—from prison—is sharing that he has found the secret to contentment: reliance on Christ.

Paul isn't telling us to compare ourselves to others, or to be like this world. He's not telling us that if we work a little harder, we can afford all those desires of our hearts. No. He's telling us that our desire should be for Christ alone and that through that—and only through that—we can find contentment; we can find blessings that are more than this world has to offer.

To me, contentment means soul-satisfying rest. When my world feels like it's spinning, I sometimes just want time to think, space, and quiet. Even when it happens, I still feel tired. I still feel like I'm spinning. Why? Because my search for rest should really be a search for contentment; a wholehearted search for Christ. Only he can provide the contentment and "rest" that comes from full reliance on his goodness, his grace, and his blessings.

Stopping Negativity in its Tracks

Does this mean that we aren't supposed to experience negativity? No. We are humans. We are prone to our own thoughts and are not always in control of them no matter what the self-improvement guru you saw on an Instagram Live may have had to say on the matter.

But—we *can* work toward alleviating it.

It starts with recognizing when we're stuck in a pattern of negativity. It might mean that we're complaining about something we can't control or just *shouldn't* be complaining about. Maybe it's an intense frustration over an unmet desire or the feeling that begins to show up when we're listening to a friend gush over a new adventure that we wish we could be a part of. If we're unable to *notice* the fact that we're drifting into a zone of negativity, we can't do much to remedy it.

Once we notice and recognize it, then we're in a position to make a difference.

First, we must ask for help. Remember: we cannot do this life alone; we are designed to be dependent. The best place to go for help and refuge is our Lord. By admitting that we're stuck in a cycle of complaint and asking him to help us find contentment, we're doing the best thing we can. We're breaking the cycle of "self" and looking up; this is mission-critical if we want to see change.

As much as we'd like to find instant remedies though, this might not be one. Can our Lord bring us contentment in a snap? Absolutely. But, we're prone to wandering. That means this needs to be a regular exercise. When we recognize that we are drifting toward the worlds of want and comparison, we must turn around. We must look up. We must ask for help.

There's something else we can work on at the same time: reframing the negative.

When we catch ourselves in cycles of negativity, we can look at the ways we are blessed. This all may sound very "first world problem-ish," and to a degree, perhaps it is. But, unless we are able to—literally—count our blessings, we have nothing but the negative to focus on.

In certain circumstances, this may be the most challenging practice possible. But, a blessing in your life might be a tiny piece of goodness that you hold onto . . . something so small you often overlook it. But, even when miniscule, that blessing is God-sent (remember, *every* good gift is from above). This means this tiny little blessing matters. What's your blessing, regardless of its size or impact? What can you shift your focus to when you find yourself in a cycle of negativity?

Lastly, we must walk away from our triggers. I'm not talking about a shallow "I'll avoid social media for awhile" or "I'll take a week off from online 'window' shopping" sort of commitment, though these may be integral parts of the process. I'm talking about fleeing from the things that make us falter.

Make no mistake: losing sight of blessings because we

cannot stop comparing ourselves to others *is* faltering.

If we're stuck in the pattern of "not having" our desires met, we cannot fix our eyes on the one who made us to be *perfectly imperfect*, designed in his image and blessed beyond measure. We cannot see that *he* is enough for us if all we can see is what we don't have, the things that are not enough.

Walking away from our triggers and running toward God requires a commitment to a lifestyle change that might look different or even strange to those around us. It might feel uncomfortable; who am I kidding, it *will* be uncomfortable. That discomfort might make it awfully tempting to call the whole thing "too hard" to justify our current choices.

Sister: Now is not the time to falter. Now is the time to go all in.

Instead of word-deep commitments that we know we'll back out of, we must go all the way. Maybe it means appointing a friend as an accountability partner to check in from time to time, or asking someone to pray with and for whatever it is you're struggling with. Joining a small group where transparency is both possible and valued. Turning off your phone when you get home from work (or before— I'm looking at you drivers who scroll on the road!). Maybe it requires signing off social media for a while or—gasp— forever. It might mean handing credit cards over to our spouses or a close friend. Or, something else entirely. Regardless, we must be willing to turn from whatever it is that is breeding discontent in our lives if we want gratitude and contentment to become our priorities.

Changing the way we see our individual worlds, asking our God for help, and noticing his blessings—big and small—are absolutely necessary to reverse glass-half-empty perspectives and attitudes.

Today is the day: it's time to start running full-speed ahead toward a glass-is-totally-full perspective that only God can provide. That means running away from whatever it is that's holding us back.

Can you take the plunge?

Questions to Consider

1. Have you caught yourself in the "negative zone?" Are there any triggers that put you there?

2. How does biblical contentment contrast with worldly contentment?

3. What could you walk away from today to help your heart grow in contentment?

4. Take the time to confess the areas of your life where you're feeling overly negative or less-than grateful. Ask for help while thanking God for the blessings he has surrounded you with today!

4

Worry Is the Opposite of Gratitude

Have you ever had those times where everything seems to be piling up around you? You can't figure out where you need to focus; you're pulled in 18 thousand directions and it feels like every part of your life is spinning?

I have. Not only that, I've seen it, and heard it from friends and even my own kids on a regular basis. Sometimes it's during times of chaos and stress: the building of a new house, a new move, a family shift or change, a new job, a lost job, an ongoing global pandemic, the opening of a new business or something else "new."

Other times, it's unexplainable. It comes out of nowhere and the root is hard to find and, still, it's debilitating.

Time and time again I've heard my friends, *especially* my girlfriends, use phrases like this (to be sure, I've used them too):

- I just don't know what to do.
- Where should I even start?
- This feels too big for me to handle.
- I can't manage this right now.
- Everything feels like it's falling/spinning/failing.

Sometimes, we call it anxiety, which it is. But, I want to be clear that I'm not discussing real, diagnosed-by-a-professional and in-need-of-proven-treatments and therapy anxiety here. Though many of us are prone to this and to depression, which should be managed and not swept under the rug, I want to steer us toward considering times of situational worry and the stress it causes. I would argue that most of us are familiar with this: when faced with uncertainties or situations that are beyond our control, our human nature is to become concerned, to look for solutions, and to worry about what's coming just around the corner.

The worst part is that when these feelings come up—when worry strikes hard—we tend to focus inward. Unlike obvious stressors or sources of drama and heartache, uncertainties and out-of-control feelings can be difficult to express or to seek validation for.

We may share our thoughts with our closest friends (or maybe we don't), but, generally, we stop there. Eventually we might find a way to take action, or to simply slop through whatever it is we're dreading, but, we never really deal with the root of it all, with the out of control mess we feel stuck in. Instead, we put it aside until, undoubtedly, it comes back up the next time things get really hard.

Make no mistake: worry has been around since the beginning of time. We—especially as women—are prone to needing to have a plan and running with it; in a way, that's probably one of our strengths! We are wranglers of chaos, keepers of schedules and managers of many things, both in our personal and professional worlds. What a gift!

But. (Notice the period there. This "but" is a big one.) When we feel unable to keep up with our innate ability to plan and schedule, when we fear what's up ahead, and when we can't focus on the here and now because of the uncertainty we're facing, we lose something important: we lose the ability to live lives of complete and total gratitude. In many ways, worry is the opposite of gratitude when you get down to the point.

Gratitude Trumps Worries

Good news: making the choice to intentionally focus on gratitude trumps worries. It's scriptural.

Philippians 4:4–9 says:

Rejoice in the Lord always; again I will say, rejoice. Let your reasonableness [in some translations: gentleness] be known to everyone. The Lord is at hand; do not be anxious about anything, but in everything by prayer and supplication with thanksgiving let your requests be known to God. And the peace of God, which surpasses all understanding, will guard your hearts and your minds in Christ Jesus.

Finally, brothers, whatever is true, whatever is honorable, whatever is just, whatever is pure, whatever is lovely, whatever is commendable, if there is any excellence, if there is anything worthy of praise, think about these things. What you have learned and received and heard and seen in me—practice these things, and the God of peace will be with you.

Read that again. Post it around your house if you think it will help (I have this on a post-it on my bathroom mirror).

Even better: memorize it. Memorize the whole chapter. I promise, it's doable. In fact, our church in DC spent the entire summer of 2020 doing just that. In the midst of current world events, completely blurry and unknown futures, and tumultuous times in our personal lives, these scriptural truths, if they take hold in your heart, are game-changing in the best possible way.

Let's break it down.

First, we're told to rejoice always, to be gentle and reasonable. But, what really stands out here, is the reminder to "not be anxious about anything."

"Hmmph," you might think. *"That's a fun goal, but come on."*

Listen. I know none of us is extremely fond of the

unicorn-and-bubbles-everything-in-the-world-is-shiny-and-perfect point of view. But please. Stick with me.

Taken one step further, we're told to pray to God about our requests *with thanksgiving.* If we do this—and if we keep our hearts and minds fixed on things that are true, honorable, just and pure—we are promised what?

Peace.

It's a cycle that should maybe look a little bit like this:

We worry (this is unavoidable. Worries crop up when we least expect them. Worrying is not sinning, but what we do with those worries can be).

We turn to God instead of spiraling. We share our worries and we praise him for *his* goodness, whether we feel like we're experiencing it right now or not. We focus on the things of this world and beyond that are undoubtedly thanks to him. We are talking about an all-consuming focus on gratitude here. Lip service won't cut it. (Remember, *every* good and perfect thing in this world is a gift from above. This is a biblical truth and fact that we often lose sight of.)

Here's where the promise really gets good.

When we do this . . . When we are CONSUMED with gratitude to our creator, our God, for every good thing in our life, we receive his peace.

Think about this repeating itself over and over again. I can't be sure, but I'm guessing that, the worries? They'll start to fade over time, replaced by our gratitude and his peace.

Can you think of a better, more relevant promise? What about anything else in this world that has nothing situational or temporary attached to it? Promises like this are rare. When we find them, we *must* pursue them wholeheartedly.

Why would we not?

It's Not an "Easy" Fix

Heart change is rarely easy. Maybe it never is. But, that seems to be what this passage in Philippians provides: a recipe of sorts for heart change, starting with gratitude and praise and ending with peace.

Once again, this passage was written to an ancient church, but it speaks loud and clear to us as believers today.

Our worries might look different, but, they require a sort of surrender, accompanied by praise, that puts God in the driver's seat of our lives.

That's what—perhaps—makes it so hard.

Remember all those traits we discussed earlier about our giftedness, as daughters of Christ, to manage schedules, make decisions and make real waves? Those are exciting things to consider; they make us feel in control of a world that often feels so far from our own grasp. Yet, we're told to hand the few things we *can,* or *think we can,* control over to someone bigger than us: someone we cannot physically see or pick up the phone to have a conversation with. Someone we must trust in a way that few other things require us to trust. This takes a change of heart that doesn't come easily. It takes time, it takes patience, it takes practice.

For the purpose of this book, it requires a shift from the world of self-interest and control to a life of abandon and full-hearted gratitude, whether we feel it at a given time or not.

It's Worth the Effort

Like other lessons from our past, though, while heart change and surrender might be hard, they're worth it.

Re-read the passage from Philippians (which won't be hard if you've gone ahead and posted it somewhere within easy view . . . ahem . . .).

If we release our concerns, cares and worries to the one who's written a plan for our lives long before the world was even created (Jeremiah 1:5, Ephesians 2:10), we are promised gifts that, regardless of our financial standing, our romantic status, our home, our career or anything else, the world cannot provide: guarded hearts and the peace of God.

In a world of influencers, of promotions, of exciting opportunities and the chasing of individual happiness, true peace, calmness and serenity are qualities hard to come by. When the world seems to be spinning around us, they might seem downright impossible. Under God's provision and care, with a focus on praise in all circumstances and continual thankfulness and gratitude, we're promised something better.

What could this mean for your life?

You might not like the answer to that question, not at first. I know I didn't.

You see, there was a season in my professional life where *everything* seemed to be going right.

I had a great job and a team that relied upon and valued me. It was a GREAT opportunity.

I also started making a name for myself in the marketing world. Suddenly, several friends in several organizations needed my help and perspective. Best of all, their organizations were willing to pay for it. I felt needed and I felt valued.

Soon, I was working my day job, then filling up another 40 hours a week on outside projects. They were fun and— at first—they were fulfilling, at least I thought they were. But soon, as they tend to do when I get over excited and over commit, things started to pile up.

My kids became extra-needy, at least, that was my initial assessment. I started falling behind in, well, everything. I became angry and stressed. Sunday nights I stopped being able to fall asleep because of what I knew the week would hold. I was on calls *all the time*. I was asked to travel out of state several times for *good* causes. Chaos is probably a light way of looking at what my life had devolved into.

Something had to change and it was going to be hard. I'm a peacemaker who wants to please everyone. Yet, in the situation I found myself, I was letting everyone down. But, making a change meant I'd have to let other people down in even bigger ways. I wavered for a long time.

During that time, as I prayed that God would help show me his will for my life, I started reading Jennie Allen's *Made for This: 40 Days to Living Your Purpose.*[1] The book was life-changing for me and I often recommend it to others (seriously: another shameless plug, check it out!), but the premise of the first day is this: we should pray for *anything.* If we are to fully surrender to God, we must give him control to do *anything* in our lives.

I prayed it, all while feeling like his purpose for my life was for me to embrace this chaos and roll with it. It made us—as a family—pretty darn financially secure and I liked the status I felt like it provided. *Sure though,* I thought, *I'll pray the prayer.*

As I dug into the study, focused hard on Philippians 4, and gave God control over *all* of my life, not just the parts I wanted to hand over, I realized the pace I was living at wasn't at all what he wanted for my life. It was hurting those around me and it was hurting my relationship with him.

As I focused on the things the verses tell us to focus on, I quickly realized that the things I was chasing on the path

---

[1] Allen, Jennie. *Made for This: 40 Days to Living Your Purpose.* W Publishing Group, an Imprint of Thomas Nelson, 2019.

I was on were not any of those things. I was bent for destruction.

One day, I gave it up. I cried. I had hard conversations. And I walked away. In a way that only God could, he made my anticipation of it all much worse than how it all actually went down.

A good friend of mine, one of my best, was actually in need of a career change, and got to step into the role I was filling, allowing her to step away from what was dragging her down, allowing her to pursue her real love and talent for brand marketing. My friendships with the contacts I needed to turn away from continued. I was able to see God more clearly in the whole unraveling, and was able to deepen my trust in him. I could spend Saturdays and evenings with my family again.

Most importantly: I was able to replace my dread, my worries, and my stresses with rejoicing—even if it meant making due with "less" in financial terms. The riches and mercies that God provided during that time of transition and letting go still bring me to tears.

Y'all . . . he was *so* good. He always has been and he always will be . . . we just need to get out of our own way sometimes.

That's the beauty in living out the commandments God has given us and dwelling with gratitude on the way he has abundantly blessed us, even if the here and now feels hard.

Is there something in your life that might be doing harm under the guise of "good" or "blessings" according to earthly standards? What could the fix look like? Are you willing to make the effort and take the chance?

Questions to Consider

1. What are you worrying about today? When was the last time the world felt like it was spinning?

2. How did you try to combat those feelings?

3. What could you have done differently? What COULD you do differently if you're currently stuck in that place?

4. How does God's promise of peace differ from what the world has to offer? How does living a life of intentional gratitude change this?

5

What Do You Dwell On?

Think about the most peaceful place in the world, somewhere you've been before. What comes to mind? Can you see it? Feel it? Tie specific scents or tastes to it? I bet you can.

Now think about a time when you experienced hurt, sadness, or another negative emotion. Can you put yourself right back there? Remember the words that were said? The feelings you felt? Probably. Right? I know I can.

This is because, as women, we have a leg up on men in the memory department. I promise. I'm not making an unfounded claim or jumping into a gender-related ability debate . . . this is backed by science. We—in general—are able to access our memories quicker, are more precise, and are more emotional when we remember or describe our memories than men.

To quote one study:

In general, females outperform males on autobiograph-
ical memory (particularly with high retrieval support via
verbal probing, random recall, story recall [and more]).[1]

It's how we are built, how we are designed by our loving
creator.

While you may feel scattered or "all over the place,"
more often than not when it comes to memory, we encode
knowledge differently than our male counterparts. It's why
we make great managers and why—when given time to sort
through details—we're also great decision-makers.

As this relates to the way we interact with our world,
especially a big world that lives at our fingertips, just a few
clicks or notifications away, this might also be a disad-
vantage.

Think about the negativity you were able to bring about
with only a quick prompt just a few paragraphs ago.

We remember a lot. When we encounter a certain message, phrase or image, it sticks with us. Sometimes it gets
filed away never to be thought of again. But, for the most
part, we remember. More than that, we dwell in those
spaces, in those memories, and we can recall them with
ease.

This goes beyond the research cited previously, but
works with it. I am willing to bet that the more we dwell on

[1] Loprinzi, Paul D., and Emily Frith. "The Role of Sex in Memory Function:
Considerations and Recommendations Int He Context of Exercise." *NCBI*, J.
Clin Med, 2018, ncbi.nlm.nih.gov.

something, the more it begins to become a part of who we are and how we move forward in these lives of ours.

When I'm surrounded by positivity after a night out with friends, I feel so much better, often it makes me feel like a weight has been lifted off of my shoulders. The same after a deep conversation with someone I haven't gotten to spend time with lately, a great date with my husband, a good laugh with one of my kids, or even a work meeting that goes well and feels productive.

On the other hand, when I feel stuck in a negative news cycle, have a conflict with a loved one, am worried about something coming just around the corner, or see something that makes me feel "less than" on social media, I'm brought lower, emotionally speaking.

My life tends to reflect whatever I happen to be pouring into it at any given time.

I'm not the only one.

We all fall into this place: what we're experiencing is the spot we stay in.

When times get really hard, or our routines get shaken completely (hello Coronavirus, world-wide unrest, and deep-rooted, serious social injustices that shake us to our very core, causing real pain to those closest to us), we must change what we dwell on. It cannot be circumstantial; it must be deeper than that.

A Company Focused on Dwelling Differently

I love to find others who point me to where I need to focus

most. Maybe they know they're doing it. Maybe they don't. Maybe it's just a friend striking up a casual conversation. But sometimes: sometimes it's the whole point.

Enter *Dwell.* Dwell is a temporary tattoo company with the mission of helping others memorize God's word. Through monthly subscription packages, this company (co-founded by our friend and the wife of a former pastor of our church), provides tattoos that spell out the first letter of each word of a given Bible verse. Along with tattoos, their packages include a devotional to focus on throughout the month, a keychain card, and more.

Sure, they're trendy. But guys, it's so much more than this. Keeping God's word close to your heart and *in* your heart, means it's likely to come to mind when you need it most. This company helps others—especially women—dwell *differently.*

I'm not saying temporary tattoos are your only option here (though I highly recommend them), but, I am saying, that if it's hard for you to focus on God's word when times get hard, or when your mind is most prone to wandering, it's time to shift your focus and try something new.

Slap on the tattoo. Keep your Bible on your nightstand and another one on your desk and another one on your kitchen counter. Set an alarm to direct you to your Bible app at a specific time each day. Play worship music filled with scriptural truth while you walk around the block and pray the words you hear back to God as you go. Post post-it's all over your mirrors and windows filled with Bible verses that you're dwelling on right now. Add a few decorative scripture passages as wall-hangings around spaces where your family spends time.

I can't say what method is right for you. But I can say that focusing on dwelling differently is critical to working on this whole grateful living thing we're working toward!

Dwelling on Scripture. Dwelling on Jesus.

It's interesting. I—maybe like many of you—grew up in the church.

When I say this . . . I mean I spent Sunday mornings, Sunday nights, and Wednesday nights there, with several other occasions during the week to show up as well. My Dad was an elder. Pastors and members of the church were often at our home for dinners, for picnics, and for other events. We vacationed with other church members and planned those vacations around VBS. I participated in Bible quizzing (if you've not sat on one of those buzzers to quickly jump on and answer questions relating to your memorization of specific passages of Scripture, I encourage you to give it a search). I went on mission trips. At age 16 I committed to going wherever it was God might send me to share his truth after I felt called to missions work in some shape or form. I was baptized to share my faith with others in a public setting at age 16 alongside some of my closest friends and my Mom.

I thought I knew who God was. I certainly knew much of his word and knew *about* him. But . . . I didn't crave it.

Somehow, I kept God at a head-deep level. I never doubted who he was or whether he was real . . . but my life wasn't shaped by his truth.

Worse, because of this head-deep knowledge, I lived in fear. I asked Jesus into my heart each and every night, terrified that during the previous times, I didn't *really* mean it or say the "right" words. I've found this situation to be common among my church-raised friends. We believed in God enough to be afraid . . . but we missed out on his grace . . . it didn't penetrate our hearts.

It wasn't until my husband and I uprooted our family to move to Asheville North Carolina and a tiny church plant downtown pastored by Chad McPhatter and Jeff Hober, that it began to change.

One day, while we were living in Pennsylvania—where we had been born and raised—my husband came home and introduced the idea slowly to me. His employer had offered him a promotion in North Carolina. While we were familiar with the beaches on the east coast of the state, we knew nothing about the mountains of Western North Carolina (WNC). We knew nothing about the hippy-loving, bluegrass mixed with other eclectic music forms on every street corner, absolutely gorgeous mountainous city called Asheville. I immediately shut the idea down.

And yet, the idea didn't go away. The offer got better. The company sent us down just to "check it out," and— maybe most importantly—John's excitement grew with the feeling that this was what we were supposed to do.

After a few months of visiting, making arrangements, and worrying constantly, we went all in, moving to a city we'd never even heard of, without a single point of contact to hold on to.

During this time of change, turmoil, and overall "newness," our new pastors encouraged and implored us to read through the Bible, cover to cover, a few chapters every single day.

What they didn't know is that we were faltering in life and in our relationship with each other. From the outside, everything looked peachy. In fact, we were complimented constantly for having it all together.

Inside though? We were cold to each other, both focused on outward things and handing each other way too many burdens to hold, burdens that weren't meant to be ours in the first place. We were angry about decisions made early in our marriage. We both felt neglected in different ways and we couldn't have felt further from each other, let alone from God.

But, we believed in God. And we believed that what our new pastors were encouraging was right.

We dove in.

Slowly, our conversations changed. We found conviction in certain areas of our life and started to think about what it was we were dwelling on.

We began to find each other again by finding truth in God's word that bound us together. We found purpose. We found reasons to be grateful. Our anger and doubts dissipated. And, it extended outward. We began to connect with our new community while leaning more heavily on one another, away from the outside influences that had impacted our early years of marriage. We realized quickly that God's word really did contain all we needed to know to get through life and to grow together.

You know what else happened?

On a personal level, I started to have a better idea of what God might be pointing me toward each day. I started—for the first time in my life—to learn how to lean into Jesus on a heart level. I started to understand that grace I mentioned I was missing earlier, while leaving my reliance on works (even though I *knew* this was the way, I somehow missed actually doing it). I started to feel the call to missional living come back, understanding that while overseas missions work may be in store for our family, I was called to share God's love wherever he planted me. The picture started to make more sense.

For clarity's sake: I'm not criticizing the pastors who shepherded me before this point. I am beyond grateful for those who encouraged me to learn scripture, to take the stories in the Bible to heart, and to help me through some of the hardest points of my life. But somehow, until Asheville, I failed to make it a habit; I cut myself short and made God a small part of my life, in his own little cubby, instead of the entire reason for my life.

Until it became a part of my life that my heart craved, I continued to dwell on the wrong things.

Once again—I will never come close to saying I've got it all together. But, the more time I spend in God's word, the more I *dwell* on his truth instead of my own circumstances. The more time I spend with him, the better I'm able to imitate him to those around me. The more I understand his grace, the more grace I'm able to extend to those around me, and to myself.

If you hear others tell you that they feel God's presence, or have felt his leading, and wonder why your experience feels "less" than that, or like your heart is having trouble latching on to it; I want to encourage you in the way Chad and Jeff did in my life and in John's life. Dig into God's word. Read it every day. Ask someone close to you to hold you accountable or to do it with you. Talk about it. Share what you're learning. When something doesn't make sense, dig for answers from God-honoring sources.

When scripture is deep down in your heart . . . imprinted on your heart . . . It changes everything.

Don't take my word—or my experience—as your model. Instead, look to scripture itself to understand the importance of dwelling on it:

- Psalm 119:11 tells us that the writer stored up God's word in his heart, that he might not sin against God.
- 2 Timothy 3:16 drives home the importance of scripture, sharing that all of it is breathed out by God and profitable for teaching, for reproof, for correction, and for training in righteousness.

- Matthew 4:4 says (in Jesus's own words) It is written, 'Man shall not live by bread alone, but by every word that comes from the mouth of God.'

That's right: the Bible itself tells us—sometimes in Jesus's words—that scriptures provide an example for everything we need in life. To various believers, this means something different, to some it means every single worship song lyric should come directly from the Bible itself.

But to me—and to all of us, regardless of our interpretation of what it means for worship or church structure—it means this: without holding tightly to God's word, and allowing it to fill our hearts, it will be nearly impossible to dwell on what he might have for our lives, and to pursue him with everything we've got.

We must dwell differently, and that starts with focusing on God's word above all else.

It might take time to become a daily endeavor. It might require changing routines, getting up earlier, turning off the TV, or staying up later. Whatever it takes, I want to encourage you to start today. Not tomorrow. Not next week. Not when life slows down (because it doesn't and we all know it). But, rather, today. I promise you, time spent in God's word is time that you will never regret. How many things in life can provide a promise like that?

Look Outside as Well

I want to be careful here: I believe the Scriptures contain

everything we need to know about God and to experience his love in our lives. They are a complete truth.

But sometimes, I find myself looking to the world around me to find God's beauty and grace.

When I look in the wrong places: i.e. social media posts. The news that gets harder to stomach every day. World events. Material possessions. And so on, I find myself wanting again (it's easy to fall here, and that's why I want to be very cautious in what I say next).

But, God gives us beauty in the here and now too, he gives us things to dwell on.

James 1:17 says that: *Every good gift and every perfect gift is from above, coming down from the Father of lights, with whom there is no variation or shadow due to change.*

As we touched briefly on in chapter three, every single good thing in this world we live in today has come down from our father in heaven, *the Father of lights.*

When my kids laugh out of pure silliness. When I get to sit on the ocean or lakeside beach (one close by, not even a dreamy white Caribbean one, though there's no denying there's beauty there too) to watch a sunrise or sunset. When I get to hike a trail that seems so far from the busyness of each day. When a conversation with loved ones feels so fulfilling and so beautiful and filled with raw honesty that I know I am both known and loved for who I am and who I was made to be. When a flower blooms after a long cold winter . . . each of these things is something my heart would consider "good." You have these experiences too, there are things—beautiful things—that are good.

That goodness might not compare to the perfect goodness that awaits me—and all of us who call on the name of our Lord to be saved—after this life is over. But, they might just give us a hint of the love our Father has for us . . . and might be a starting point of something that we can dwell on—in concurrence with Scripture, not as substitute—that give us small things to be grateful for and to reflect on as we work on increasing our gratitude and shifting our perspective.

When you're struggling, start small. Start with thinking about what you dwell on, and what you could shift your focus toward. Are their simple pleasures that you can attribute to God as you begin to dig deeper into his word. Are there things, places, or memories that allow you to feel his beauty, his grace, and his might?

What simple thing can you recognize as good and thank God for, right here, right now? What ripple effect could this cause in your life that could draw you closer to him?

On what *do* you dwell? On what *should* you dwell?

Questions to Consider

1. Be honest with yourself. In your free time, what do you find yourself dwelling on? What sort of cycle does this create for you (worry, anxiety, gratitude, specific behavior)?

2. Is reading the Bible a part of your daily routine? If not, what's holding you back?

3. Why is reading Scripture so important for changing your heart?

4. Can you commit or recommit to diving into God's word, even for a few minutes each day? When will you make the time? Who can you ask to hold you accountable as you jump into your new routine?

6

Are You Humble?

"If I must boast, I will boast of the things that show my
weakness."

– 2 Corinthians 11:30

God has built his church around and through communities.

Yes, we exist to be in personal relationships with him,
and to follow his leading for our lives and the lives of our
families. But, he's also given us each other.

When Jesus was here on Earth, he did his ministry surrounded by others. He lived with them, traveled with them,
and conversed with them. I'm willing to bet that during
their "down times," the everyday parts of their lives that
aren't documented in scripture, that they did what many
of us do: they shared stories. They reminisced. They found

common ground. They laughed. They disagreed. They did life together and faced hurdles together.

We do the same.

This all continued after he rose from the grave and ascended back into heaven. His church came together as a community of individuals that did life corporately. They ate together, broke bread together, and worshipped the Lord together. They pooled finances—whatever that looked like back then—and resources to ensure everyone in their communities were taken care of.

They showed up for one another time and time again. When one suffered, they all did. When one succeeded, they all did. When one needed support, or uplifting news, they did what they could.

When friends who don't believe ask me what the church is supposed to look like, or what church means to me— that's where I go. I'm not sure there's a more beautiful vision for what the church of God is supposed to look like than what we find in the book of Acts.

Can you?

Here in our family, my favorite memories—regardless of the home in which they took place—often involve our kids, our family members, our neighbors, or our good friends surrounding our kitchen island or deck table, just enjoying each other and sharing everyday ups and downs. Sometimes that means side-splitting laughter. Sometimes it means challenging conversations. Sometimes it means tears, hugs. Sometimes it means silence and deep mourning. But it *always* involves transparency and a willingness to be real. If we can't let our guards down, those experiences can't penetrate the surface. Our experiences would be lacking depth.

But somewhere along the line, around the time our lives became more digital than "in-person . . ." we forgot about the humility that's required to break down barriers and grow. We lost real, in-person community that is designed to be such a blessing in our lives.

We lost humility. We started boasting about what we have more than confessing what we don't have. We started living for the outside world, the world that doesn't gather around our kitchen islands and outdoor firepits.

It's okay: We're not lost forever . . . not yet. But, we may require a mindset adjustment or several. This likely applies to most of us, not just a select few.

An Open Door as a Starting Point

Growing up, there weren't many TV shows that were permitted in my home. But, one that always seemed to be on was Full House. Many of those episodes are fondly burned into my memory, along with other flashbacks from the "good old days."

So naturally, when Netflix and the original cast of Full House came together for a sequel series, Fuller House, I (much to the chagrin of my husband) was *all in.*

I loved the way it would tie in fond memories from the original series, and got a kick out of the "cheesier" laughs that come from clean family fun and a little new drama. But something else caught my attention as well: whenever there was a knock at the front door, the response from whoever was inside was always the same, "Door's always open!"

See, that's something I remember from childhood: our door was always open. I remember my mom sitting around the kitchen table with any number of friends or younger women from the church who looked to her for advice or a listening ear. I could confidently ask that a friend come over at almost any time, or that a cousin come to spend the night, fairly sure the answer would be yes. We lived life in the open.

We've tried to set up our home—whether in Pennsylvania, North Carolina, or most recently, Virginia—to be the same. Sure, when the COVID pandemic set in, those gatherings became fewer and farther between—and mostly outdoors when they were possible—but here's the thing: when face-to-face conversations become less prominent in our lives, we tend to focus less on the needs of others, and more on what we have and don't have. It becomes easier to hide the rough patches we're facing, replacing them with false pictures of perfection that—if we're honest—often leave us focusing on what we don't have or what we desire.

Just as damaging, they often also cause the same reaction in others. When everyone thinks everyone else has it all together, it's a lot easier to dive into the negative cycle that begins when we start to play the comparison game.

The global pandemic made this trend even more apparent. Suddenly we all had—and maybe still even as the world reopens and figures out what comes next, have—a lot more time to focus on what we don't have while boasting about what we do have.

Humility somehow lost its appeal.

Should We Stop Sharing?

What does this mean? That we should stop sharing?

I don't think that's the case. The Bible tells us we are to let our lights shine for others (Matthew 5:15–16). In fact, it tells us that when we let our lights shine for others, they can better glorify God.

But, perhaps a motivation check is a good starting point.

I mean it: you've got to be real with yourself, we all do. And sometimes, we'll learn things we don't want to learn.

When I was in that destructive period of my life that I mentioned earlier, it was fun to share progress. I lost 95 pounds; who doesn't want to share something like that? Friends encouraged me to start a blog—unaware of the lengths I was going to in order to achieve these results. So, I went all-in. After all, I was doing it to help others.

At least, that's what I told myself.

But on the side, I was obsessively checking the stats after each and every post. I was relishing the compliments. I was taking each photo I shared 10–30 times, not wanting the wrong angle to show. My effort that was meant to "help" and "encourage" others sure mattered a lot to me . . . and centered around me as well. In fact, I built a whole network under the guise of helping others that helped feed my own need for self-worth, all while I was wrecking my health and my relationship with my husband.

Ooof. It still hurts to talk about if I'm honest. If I'm extra honest, it also hurts to look at photos from that period in my life. My reliance and my confidence was centered around all the wrong things . . . and I was loving it.

Maybe your motivation is different. Maybe you feel like you're stumbling across the finish line that is the end of each day, and desperately want to feel like you seem to have it all together. Maybe your anxiety has you spiraling and you can't put your finger on why, but, the image you've constructed to share on the outside gives you just a tiny bit of control. Maybe you're struggling financially and don't want others to know how hard you're fighting to keep the house you're so proud of.

No matter what it is, there's a second level that might not feel obvious quite yet: perhaps in your boasting under the guise of smiles and all the right angles, you just want to be known.

Known Doesn't Mean Famous

When I say "known," I don't mean famous. While that may be a motivating factor, I mean something deeper.

As humans, we crave strong relationships. Remember: God designed community for a purpose and tells us numerous times that when we function together, we all function better for his glory. Science confirms this: stronger relationships lead to lower levels of depression and anxiety, higher overall levels of health, and longer lives.[1]

Interesting that many of these benefits mirror those that are linked to living lives full of intentional gratitude, isn't it? *Perhaps we're on to something . . .*

Yet, the more our lives shift to a more public, online setting, the more we're tempted to boast in the best parts of our lives while hiding the parts that need attention that can only come to light from places of deep humility.

Our #blessed sharing habits have actually inhibited our ability to connect with our communities. They've helped us hide our real selves while giving us reason (whether real or exaggerated) to humblebrag about the good things. They've allowed us to close our doors to those we need most, who also need us most, while hiding the light that God has placed in our hearts.

But if we acknowledge this . . . and we see it for what it is; we can change it. We can take off our filters. We can share like we've been too intimidated to do in the past. And if we do? Those around us might just feel free to do the same. Think of the ripple effect this sort of intentionality could create!

---

[1] "The Health Benefits of Strong Relationships." *Harvard Women's Health Watch.* Harvard Health Publishing. Harvard Medical School, 6 Aug. 2019. Web. 11 Nov. 2020.

Don't Worry: There's Hope

Do you know what I love most about the Bible?

While it brings to light our inability to get through this life on our own, and our dependence on God that was so great that he had to send his son to reconcile us to himself, the most basic pattern is this: God ALWAYS shows up.

Think about it . . .

David has an affair with a married woman, gets her pregnant, tries—and fails—to hide it, then has her husband killed? God shows up, delivering his own son through David's bloodline and calling David a man after his own heart.

A woman who is accused of adultery is brought before Jesus as a test by the Pharisees, who know that the law gives them the right to stone her? Jesus tells them that if any of them is without sin, he can cast the first stone. While he challenges her to "go and sin no more," fully acknowledging her past wrongs, he also demonstrates complete forgiveness, saves her life, and changes her heart in the process.

Peter denies Jesus three times during the crucifixion? Jesus chooses him to become the "rock" upon which he would build the church.

Our problems might seem lesser than some of the more well-known Bible characters (maybe they don't, struggles are hard and we all have a knack for getting ourselves into some pretty big disasters), but, in this world—especially within our generation—a lack of humility has almost been given a free pass, even though the scriptures are clear on this topic.

God's grace makes lives that reflect humility possible. Yet, we often overlook it somehow. We prefer to lean on guilt, furthering the "I'll never measure up" narrative we've been exploring throughout this book . . . the place we find ourselves in more than we'd like to admit.

God loves us. He sent his son to die for us. If we believe in him and choose to turn toward and follow him, his grace covers our sins in a way no action we could take on our own ever could.

He draws near to us as we draw near to him. He pursues us wholeheartedly. He simply asks us to turn around, re-directing our focus onto him. It was true in scripture, it's true today. Grace wins. Full stop.

If our lives don't demonstrate hearts changed by and reliant on total and complete grace, we're boasting in the wrong thing and our lights aren't bringing others to the feet of Jesus.

Remember: God always shows up. Yes. It requires in-tentional effort on our part, not in a "works" over faith sort of way, of course, but rather a decision to make him the Lord of our hearts. Yes, it requires heart-change, humility, and accountability. But y'all: the truth remains. Humble hearts will change this world of ours. Humble attitudes will attract the communities that God desires we participate in.

Humble hearts will allow us to live lives that center on gratitude first.

Let's commit to searching our hearts, and asking God to do the same. Let's be transparent. Let's ask God to use us how he sees fit, not in ways that bring us attention in all the wrong ways.

Questions to Consider

1. Look back at your last 20 social media posts. Think through each one and consider the "why" behind each. How did the reactions, the likes, the comments, you received make you feel?

2. What purpose do you see for yourself in the communities in which you participate (both in-person and online)?

3. What are you struggling with? What are you hiding from others? Is God asking you to be transparent? What's holding you back?

4. In what do you boast? Read through 1 Peter 5:1–11. Why does God charge us with humility? Why should you cast your anxieties on him? Ask him to bring heart change in this area if you are struggling.

5. Who makes up your community? Can you take away the filters to be real with them? How could you make an effort to be more transparent today?

7

Pay Attention to Your Story

Remember It Isn't Really Yours

I've had plans / Shattered and broken /Things I have hoped in / Fall through my hands / You have plans / To redeem and restore me / You're behind and before me / Oh, help me believe / God You don't need me / But somehow You want me / Oh, how You love me / Somehow that frees me / To take my hands off of my life / And the way it should go.

– Tenth Avenue North, "Control"

Sometimes it feels as though we're pre-programmed to be planners. We dream dreams about what's to come, we create our calendars for the next week, we plan our vacations and job promotions for the next five years. We ask our kids what they want to be when they grow up as if they can know these things with certainty when they're five. We document it all and build memory banks around the highpoints in our lives.

But, what if instead of looking forward, we took a second to look back. I don't mean only looking back at the highpoints, I mean taking stock of it all.

Maybe you'll be surprised by what you find. Maybe you'll find an important piece to the intentional gratitude puzzle.

Stick with me here.

What's Your Story?

Before our family uprooted to North Carolina, our pastor was Pastor John. He had a no-nonsense, straight-shooting personality that allowed for complete honesty in conversations. I always appreciated that he put up with no half answers or false smiles. If life was hard, you could share with him or not, but pretending all was good was a no go.

Something that I will never forget about Pastor John, was that, along with this no-nonsense personality, he broke down walls with strangers (restaurant servers, church visitors, and beyond) from the first conversation onward. In fact, the first time someone met him, the first question he asked was generally "What's your story?"

I have to admit, I was caught off guard when I was faced with this question during our first meeting at the back of the sanctuary following a Sunday morning church service. I mean, do we really think things like this through in advance when we don't know the question is coming? I sure didn't.

Armed with normal first-time greeting information—where I attended college, what I was studying, who was a part of my family there at the church—I realized I didn't actually have an answer to that question that I knew how to share. Sharing an answer to a question like that requires reflection, thought, and—if we're honest—some vulnerability.

But wow, what a way to get people thinking.

When I think about my story, I think about adoption as a starting point, and something that's woven throughout every chapter—something I write about frequently as it helped shape who I am, how I connect with those around me, and how I parent. It's something that caused many questions, forcing me to come face to face with some things that others don't often have to consider. It's also shown a love so much greater than anything I could ever script myself . . . a love that took on many forms. My birth mother choosing to put me in the arms of another family able to provide to me in ways that she could not was the ultimate act of sacrificial love. My parents waiting with open arms (even with hurting hearts) was the ultimate act of acceptance and demonstration of Christ's love for those of us who could never do anything to deserve it. This balance has always been something I've walked between, grateful at ALL times for what it meant for my parents and my birth mother. I can't think of my story without thinking about this.

I think about the church, and how I always felt God close to me, even when I chose to run in my own direction. I never doubted choosing him . . . though the pain I caused my own heart and his during the times I felt as though I deserved some more of what the world told me would be amazing is something I had to reckon with in full-hearted surrender and repentance. I think about those who were waiting with open arms, devoid of all judgement, when I was ready to turn back.

I think about John—we've been together for over half of our lives at this point. I think about the early days when we felt destined for destruction as we lived for ourselves and caused some significant hurt.

I think about frustration, about starting over, about our careers, about becoming a family.

But most of all, I think about the way God claimed me as his own, and used every single part of my story to draw me into his story. I see how he wove relationships together in ways that I could have never imagined. In how he brought healing to hurting hearts. In how he used specific situations to quite literally rescue me from certain doom. I see that in every single situation I've encountered, even when I was running away from him, he was running before, behind, and alongside me.

You see, he was writing my story, using every plotline for his ultimate glory, in ways I may not ever understand during my time on Earth. When I fall into this spiral of reflection that looks at the way he has worked in my heart and in my life from the time I was born until today, no matter how much certain chapters sting, something magical (at least, I consider it to be magical), happens: I overflow with gratitude.

Sometimes, it's so real I can feel it and am brought to tears by how magnificent it feels (even when life is really, really hard).

When I feel weighed down by the unknowns of what's to come, and when the tension in the world surrounding me feels so palpable that I think I could crumble from it, reflecting on the fact that God has worked in my life from the start allows me to know with certainty that he won't stop now.

I may not like or enjoy the outcome. I might not understand it. It might hurt. But guys, if we acknowledge that God—the God who promises to use all things and circumstances for his glory—is the author of our stories, we start to step out of the cycle of self. We start to overflow with a gratitude that comes straight from our hearts.

It might not look like surface gratitude for material things, or a great vacation, or a really great hair day. It might not even be for something the world tells us is "good." Instead, it's a deep gratitude that helps us reframe the way we see the world around us and allows us to focus upward, out of whatever mess we feel as though we've created for ourselves.

It's Your Turn

I'm sure you've reflected on the past. We're all pretty good at it.

But, have you ever taken the time to sit down and think through your whole story? If I were to ask you the same question Pastor John asked everyone he met, how would you respond?

Maybe on the surface you just feel like shoulder shrugging when you consider your story in comparison with others—many of us don't have drastic, dramatic conversion stories or epic life events. That's okay. Maybe it's even wonderful. It doesn't mean you don't have a story, it just means maybe Jesus has been a part of it longer than others (there is beauty in this!).

Take the time to sit down and draft it out. Start at the beginning. Don't skip the hurts: they're part of who you are. The mistakes? Make sure they're in there too.

Then, go deeper. Look for things that felt like coincidences at the time, but turned into bigger situations and stories than you ever thought possible. Think about "chance" meetings that led to conversations or actions that changed who you are today.

Most importantly, ask God to help you see the way he was working in your story, and to reveal how it's brought you to where you are today.

This is no small undertaking. It might mean thinking about subjects you try to avoid. It might mean dealing with things you would rather not deal with (heart work is hard!). But, as you start to put the pieces—the shiny ones and the broken ones—together, look at the beauty that comes from the uniqueness of your story.

Here's where it gets *really* exciting.

Gratitude will start to emerge. It might not be for things that feel really great, and it might not mean being grateful for pain, but, instead, it might be better. It might just show you that God has been right there with you through it all. Better yet, it might allow you to trust him in a new way, a way that makes the anxieties and fears of tomorrow feel just a little less overwhelming.

When we start to see our individual stories as God's collective, singular story, we cannot move forward in the same way we did before. We begin to see gratitude as the only appropriate reaction, and we begin to trust like we never have before. That, friends, is a gift.

You Might Need to Make Things Right as a First Step

There's a chance—maybe a really big chance—that certain parts of your story still need some resolving.

Once again: I want to be clear—when I say "make things right," I don't mean on your own. Remember, we're talking about how God writes and uses our stories. This means that if we've gotten ourselves somewhat off track, we'll need his help to get back on track. If you aren't at the point where you can find a way to be grateful—at all—for ANY part of a particular part of your story, chances are you may be holding on to something that needs some fixing.

I'm not sure what you're holding on to. Pride that makes you feel better than or above others, or a different kind of pride that hides your need for dependence on others. Anger about a hurt you've experienced at someone else's hands. Shame at a hurt you've caused that hasn't yet been resolved—or maybe even come to light yet. Self-esteem issues that leave you focused on your body or your capabilities, that stop you from seeing you were created beautifully in God's own image, putting a wedge between you and God *and* likely, you and others. Fear about a situation that's completely out of your control. An addiction to a behavior (shopping) or a substance (medications, drugs, alcohol, that nightly glass of wine that you're not sure you can do without).

Whatever it is, whether it falls into one of those categories or not, when things are unresolved *that have the ability to be resolved* (for some clarity here: some things naturally take time and there's no way around it), they can be hard to see past. Finding gratitude when pain is raw can be a challenge. We are still called to practice it and to get intentional, but, if we take steps to resolve the things that are keeping us from God and his plan for the next chapter in our lives, then we need to make them right.

This might mean taking real steps to humble yourself, revealing secrets that you've hidden deep from others. It might mean an awkward conversation and some apologizing that may or may not be accepted. It might be offering forgiveness to the person that's hurt you most. It might mean finally handing a situation over to God and leaving it in his hands, instead of grabbing control again. It might mean getting a professional involved. It might even mean medication that you're not sure how others—or yourself— will feel about.

There are a couple points worth mentioning right here and now:

1. Anything that you're struggling with is already known. There's nothing about who you are today, what you've done in the past, or what you'll face in the future that our father in Heaven doesn't already know about.

2. There's nothing that you could ever do that will change the way God sees and values and loves you. You are his. You were bought with a price so steep yet given so willingly, even while you were fully known before you ever came to be. You. Are. Loved. Period. Even better? Repentance takes the weight off your shoulders, allowing you to connect deeper with your Savior. Is there anything sweeter?

3. Getting right with others doesn't always guarantee the outcome you're hoping for. It does, however, allow you to let go of whatever you're holding on to, while fully embracing whatever it is God has for you going forward. We can't control others and there's no way around it. But, we can be grateful for what we learn and take steps toward resolution, even if they hurt in the here and now.

There's something sweet here. In just a few more pages, we'll get to how you can use the story God has written for your life to bless, love, and encourage others.

Here's the beauty, the sweet, epically life-changing beauty: when you've asked for forgiveness and given whatever sin you're holding on to—whether you're ready to admit you're doing so or not—there's a realization that you've made your heart right before the God who created *the universe.* Every single part of it. Every star. Every speck of sand. Every mountain. Every distant galaxy (which, by the way, scientists don't even know if they'll ever know the count of. Dwell on that for a minute!). He already knows about it and he's already there to love you through it. By giving your struggles, your shame, your sin to him, what do you have to hide from anyone? You can move forward knowing this constant, unchanging love is always on your side (whether you repent or not, it's true, though it may be harder to feel when you're in the deep end).

Nothing in this world can separate you from this love. What a magnificent promise. What a brilliant starting point for gratitude!

If you need to make things right with someone, or with God, right now is an excellent time to get moving. Remember: you are not alone, nothing you're feeling right now changes this fact.

Using Your Story

If you've just started this process of deep diving into your past, you might not be ready to shout it from the rooftops. You may need to take time to process it all. You might need to talk to someone, a pastor, a counselor, your small group etc., or take any number of the steps above that we've just discussed.

But, as you begin to see your past as a testimony of God's working in and through the everyday circumstances of your life, and you begin to use that as the foundation for how you move forward, it changes everything.

It also helps you better connect with those around you.

Remember, as we discussed in the last chapter, we grow together by sharing our stories; they help us connect.

When your life begins to revolve around gratitude for what God has done in and through you, and you begin to trust fully in his plans for your future, sharing your story becomes a natural next step, helpful for deepening your own faith, and encouraging others, which we will get to shortly.

Your story is directly related to your life, but the Bible tells us it's also purposefully crafted to do much more:

- In Philippians 1:14, Paul shares that because of [his] chains, most of the brothers in the Lord [were] encouraged to speak the word of God more courageously and fearlessly.
- In Psalm 78:4, we're told to not hide our stories from our children, but to tell the next generation of the glorious deeds of the Lord, his power, and the wonders that he has done.

- In Luke chapter 8, Jesus heals a man tormented by demons. When the man begs to go with Jesus, Jesus instead tells him to "Return home and tell how much God has done for you."

When we are intentional in searching for God's working in our stories, when we get serious about practicing gratitude for the highs and the lows, and when we start using it as the foundation for the way we live life and the way we connect with others, we become living, breathing testimonies with a purpose much deeper than any plans we could craft for our own lives. Every day becomes an opportunity to praise more, trust deeper, and connect differently. Isn't this the sort of "blessed" our hearts really crave?

Who can you share your story with? Who needs to hear of the way God has worked in your heart and renewed your spirit?

Ask God to open doors and to lead you to others who might need you to share. Remember, there's a reason for your story. There is meaning to be found, and meaning to share!

Questions to Consider

1. What's your story? Think about how you would answer that question and consider writing it down. Then, think more. Pray. Walk away from it for a while. Come back. Take your time: your story matters, it may be exactly what helps your heart draw nearer to our God, or, what brings others to his feet.

2. As you consider your story, where do you see evidence of God's faithfulness?

3. Are their unresolved hurts that are blocking your ability to fully rely on God's faithfulness, or to live with gratitude? How can you move forward? Who can you ask to help in this endeavor?

8

Keep It Simple

Living Minimally

With recent changes we have experienced in this world, we've been given a collective opportunity to look at life differently (and to consider how we move forward). As various parts of our world experienced a lockdown of one sort or another during the COVID-19 pandemic, we've been able to spend a lot more time thinking and reflecting.

This can—for the most part—go one of two ways.

The first, is to complain about the changes to our everyday way of life, to see how we used to live, the luxuries we used to take for granted, and to long deeply to return to the past. Often, this train of thought is accompanied by frustration, fear, and tension.

The second, is to look at where we are now, and to appreciate the basics: our health, a society that allows us access to what we need most (even if it's a little more in-convenient than before the whole world changed with the COVID pandemic and all the subsequent events), and to focus on making the most of the here and now. When we see others leaning into this way of thinking, we often observe peace and—surprise—gratitude.

Before going any deeper here, I want to be clear: change, especially forced change, is *hard*. Trust me. When our world shut down in March of 2020, I didn't take the news with as much grace as I wish I could have. We all have our moments, and that's okay.

The point is to notice the difference, and to try to change when necessary (and, of course, to ask God to help us see where those changes must begin and to guide us along the way).

We—All of Us—Are Extremely Blessed

Here we go again with that tricky "blessed" term. Don't eye roll just yet though, alright?

Maybe when you were young, you were guilted with the "there are starving kids in Africa" rant when you didn't clean your plate, or, you complained about your dinner choices. But, team, the sentiment behind that rant is true.

In fact, nearly half of our world (over three billion people) really do live on less than $3 a day. Over one billion cannot access clean water. Basic sanitation? That's a pipe dream for over two billion humans on our planet.

I'm not here to guilt-trip you. Let's face it, some people

in our country *do* have it much easier than others when it comes to material things and many, many of those around are struggling just to get by—this may be true of your life today. But, when we look at the basics; for the most part, if we have running water in our homes and something to eat every day, we're off to a pretty great start.

When we play the comparison game we mentioned earlier, however, or, when we start to dwell on the information influencers would have us view as "reality," we don't do ourselves any favors.

It's time to step back, evaluate, and forge a new path forward.

Which Brings Us to Simplicity

For me, this all came to a shocking reality during our family's "move" to Washington D.C.

In December of 2019, John accepted a position in D.C. that we firmly felt God had put in our path (much like during our earlier relocation to Asheville, North Carolina). But, we didn't really feel his loosening on our grip of our home in here Pennsylvania. It didn't make a lot of sense, in fact, it was extremely confusing and at many points frustrating. But, we decided to move forward with trust.

We found a home to rent in McLean, Virginia, and set up a minimal home that covered all the basics, while maintaining the household in Pennsylvania, so the kids could finish out the school year and we could figure out exactly what we needed to do.

While we had no idea the world was about to shift, God sure did. We are convinced he didn't allow us to feel free of PA because we would need to use it as a home base during the time of COVID-19.

It also provided us an outlet to start to head down to DC to acclimate a bit, spending weekends in a home with the bare essentials, no internet, and extra time with family. An added blessing was different walls to stare at while stores, restaurants, and museums were out of the question.

On one of these visits, something really interesting hit me. Honestly, it shook me to my core.

I love things. If I'm honest about where I struggle with the comparison game and with everything related to gratitude, it's that I like nice things. I also like mementos of past events and travel. In fact, at the time, our home in Pennsylvania was almost a shrine to memories and adventures that I thought helped build our family.

During one of our weekends though, as I was sitting on a couch that didn't quite feel "homey" yet, in a home with bare walls (we didn't want to put nails in a wall in a rented home), I realized that I had everything I needed. In fact, I realized that I could put every part of our PA home in storage, and continue living a very minimal lifestyle, one without the "things" we'd been acquiring during our 11 years of marriage, and that my heart could still find contentedness. Just like that, God began to release my hold on PA, helping me transfer my reliance on things of this world, to him, and freeing us—as a family—to follow him fully into whatever he would lead us toward going forward.

As I'm working on this chapter, I still don't know what it all means. We're still living between two places, unsure of the big plan, yet willing to follow and trying to be faithful to whatever it is God may be calling us to. And while I often lean on and depend upon certainties in life, the peace that comes with knowing *I can* let go when God decides it's time, allows me to move forward with confidence. My hope is not in things, as much as my heart often desires them. It's in a great God who has a purpose for all things.

There's no hope greater than this!

I had heard many sermons and adages about leaving the things of this world behind, but, for some reason, it never clicked. It took a complete shift in lifestyle, and a forced period of "slowing down" and refocusing for me to see that the blessings God has bestowed upon me have nothing to do with material things. Yes. They're nice. Yes, God has been generous. But my worth in him has absolutely nothing to do with any of it.

Does this idea of minimal living hit your heart? Is simple something exciting to you? Or, is it unsettling, upsetting, or even terrifying? You may not be called to change anything in this area. However, if the thought of an about-face when it comes to "things" feels off-setting, some evaluation may be necessary. Where's your focus? Where does your peace come from?

Another note to add here is this: minimal living may have nothing to do with things, though that is often the easiest example to come up with. Minimal living may mean cutting back on the busyness of your schedule to make time for the things God wants to fill your time with—time to listen to him, impromptu conversations with neighbors, heart-filled conversations with your kids, or something else all together. It might mean saying no to the fifth activity for your third kid in the same season. It might mean setting aside a day that remains free each week, open to whatever God may will to fill it with. It might mean stepping away from social media for a day or for a week or more to stop the constant stream of information and conversation you find yourself immersed in. Minimal living sometimes has nothing at all to do with material goods.

When we live simple lives, filled with intentional gratitude, our worth in Christ can better come into focus.

And, That Worth Is Great Beyond Measure

When we are stuck in the day to day, understanding the worth we have in simply being children of God can be awfully challenging, especially when we are feeling "less-than," or like no matter how hard we work and strive, we still can't make ends meet.

But, our thoughts don't make the way God sees us and what he says about us any less true.

In case you need a reminder, here are a few verses— pieces of biblical truth that are unchanging and constant— to focus on:

- Psalm 139:13–16: For you formed my inward parts; you knitted me together in my mother's womb. I praise you, for I am fearfully and wonderfully made. Wonderful are your works; my soul knows it very well. My frame was not hidden from you, when I was being made in secret, intricately woven in the depths of the earth. Your eyes saw my unformed substance; in your book were written, every one of them, the days that were formed for me, when as yet there was none of them.
- Genesis 1:27: So God created man in his own image, in the image of God he created him; male and female he created them.
- Ephesians 2:10: For we are his workmanship, created in Christ Jesus for good works, which God prepared beforehand, that we should walk in them.
- Jeremiah 31:3: I have loved you with an everlasting love; therefore I have continued my faithfulness to you.

God made us in his image and by his design. He has written every day of our life from before we were born. He tells us this in Scripture so it is true. We are his workmanship. We. Are. Loved.

It also means that in love, God didn't make a mistake. Your faults and shortcomings? They are a part of who you are, but they are not an accident. We are valued by our creator and have been before we ever came to be. When we fall short, he makes a way to get back on track—even if it takes some pain along the way.

Remember this when life is heavy and hard and gratitude is hard to come by.

Let us find our worth in God's truth and love, a love so deep that he sent his own son to redeem and save us and bring us back to him. Not in what the world says we should chase or desire. Let us be grateful for this simple truth.

If this is where our worth is found, and this is where we find gratitude, then simple living with God at the center of each day is enough. What a refreshing promise.

A Note about the Role of Surrender in Gratitude

As we progress on this journey of gratitude and consider the role of living simply, it's important to think about how surrender plays into all of it.

There is a wonderful song by All Sons & Daughters called "I Surrender." The lyrics go like this:

The riches of this world will fade
The treasures of our God remain
Here I empty myself to owe this world
Nothing and find everything in You
I surrender, I surrender
I surrender all to You
Take my life, a sacrifice
In You alone I'm satisfied
Here I empty myself to owe this world
Nothing and find everything in You

Everything in You
I surrender, I surrender
I surrender all to You

It's funny. I—and maybe you too—have sung songs about surrender my whole life. I "get" that I'm supposed to surrender my desires and will to that of God's. But, until recently it didn't make sense, not fully at least. Not until John and I started truly trying to allow God to be the center of our lives, the basis of all decisions, and our compass for how we walk through this world.

As we did, our church started including this song in Sunday worship. And one week, it brought me to my knees, quite literally. In fact, I wrote the words in the back of my Bible because of the profound impact they made on my heart.

I often find myself fighting God. I'm not one who struggles to feel his tugging on my heart. When I've been running away from him I have always felt him pulling me close. I've never doubted: that's not where I have a hard time. This is something I am literally eternally grateful for. I know this isn't true of all of us.

That doesn't mean there's no struggle in my life and in my heart.

My struggle comes in allowing him to actually lead after I feel that tugging.

Yes, God, I know you want me to listen to the call John is feeling on his heart right now. I feel the call, too. But

God, I feel like we're just starting to put down roots again. I PLANTED FLOWERS HERE. Please don't make me give them up. I want to reach your people HERE, not THERE.

That right there friends, is an actual conversation I had with God (at least, a pretty spot-on summary), over a 6–month period that we felt God leading John to take a role in DC, that might introduce us to a wider range of cultures, and give us the experience we felt like he might want to use to further our call into missional living that still could lead us overseas one day.

When I start to have those thoughts, I try to pull God's will into mine, instead of surrendering my will to him. I start to owe this world something, instead of owing God everything. I stop living gratefully and start holding on for dear life to things that I was never supposed to hold onto in the first place.

Do you see the shift?

When I—instead—start surrendering my will and life to God's plan for it, whatever it might be, I can thank him for everything he's placed there. When I'm too focused on holding on to what I'VE built, I lose the ability to thank him for what HE'S built.

Living simply helps me place my treasures back in God's hand. It helps me thank him with a full heart, instead of empty words. This is true for all of us. Surrender is a universal need . . . which means it is also a universal struggle.

If you're struggling to simplify a life, or lifestyle, that you've worked hard for, or are struggling to let your life align with God's will, or are finding it hard to be grateful for what you're facing right now (I get it), I recommended practicing surrender. Focus on the words of the song above, and make them the prayer of your heart.

Unsure of whether or not you're in need of surrender? Pray out loud or write down the most honest prayer you can, what you feel in your heart: your greatest fear, your most anxious thought, the things you haven't ever shared with anyone. What do you hear or see? Reliance on God? Or, reliance on yourself and this world?

The exercise isn't meant to be critical or to promote negative self-thinking. It's meant to open our eyes to things God might be putting his finger on in our lives, begging us to surrender them to him.

Simplicity, surrender, and gratitude cannot be separated; they're critical for making the most of God's plan for our lives. Don't pass up his eternal treasure to build something that will never last. I promise—and more importantly, the Bible promises—that leaning into him will be the greatest daily decision you make on this side of Heaven.

Questions to Consider

1. Do you find yourself grateful for what you have, or longing for what you don't have more often? How can considering your basic blessings help shift this way of thinking?

2. How does simple living help us live with intentional gratitude?

3. In what way can you start to depend less on what others tell you is essential, to refocus on what is essential? What areas of your life could you begin to minimalize?

4. How does God define your worth? How does this truth change the things you chase?

5. What are you struggling to surrender? How can you give up whatever it is you're clinging tightly to? Why should you take this step? Ask God to help in this endeavor: you don't have to go at it alone!

9

Be Bold

It's Okay to Reach for Your Dreams

When we talk about living with intentional gratitude that's centered on God's goodness, his grace, and his plan for our lives, it's vastly different from the gratitude that we see blasted on mainstream media, promoted by self-help gurus, and shared by well-meaning friends and family, as we've touched on throughout this book so far.

This kind of gratitude requires real effort on our part, and a willingness to look at our world through a different view than we may have grown accustomed too, but it also relies a lot on looking upward more than inward. We will talk more about what intentional gratitude looks like in action in the next chapter, but, right now it's important to make another point about all of this.

The other point is this: relying totally on God, and

choosing to see his blessings in our life before we see anything else does not mean that we should stop chasing our
dreams, or, live with timidity.

Through scriptures, we are told time and time again to
be bold and courageous:

- In Joshua 1:9, we are told that *strength and courage*
  are actually commanded of us.
- In Ephesians 3:12, we're told to *approach God with
  boldness and confidence.*
- In 2 Corinthians 3:12, we learn that our hope
  should enable *boldness.*
- In Acts 4:13, *boldness* is proof that someone had
  spent time with Jesus.

Throughout all of God's word, it becomes quite clear
that boldness is commanded and expected of us.

Do we practice this kind of boldness? Do we use it as a
measuring stick for our level of reliance on God verses reliance on ourselves? Or, do we give it a nice little nod and
move on with our days, holding on to our own perspectives,
needs, fears and thoughts?

When I think this through, I know my answer is that my
boldness isn't always the first quality that comes to mind
when I evaluate my current situation. What about you?

How Boldness Begins with Gratitude

So, what's the link? How does gratitude connect to boldness?

It's simple: when we make gratitude to God for his grace and his goodness the central focus of our lives, we stop putting ourselves first. We learn quickly that our reliance is on him first and above all else. When we trust fully in his intentions and plans for our lives—as the verses above and many, many others demonstrate—we are able to live boldly. We're able to walk in a way that looks different to those around us and brings glory to God instead of ourselves.

When you look at it this way, gratitude becomes foundational to being an imitator of Christ, helping us approach situations we find ourselves in with confidence—boldness—that is truly not of this world.

What a revolutionary way to walk forward. Think about the implications of this kind of forward motion!

God's Boldness May Look Different than the World's Boldness

As women, we get conflicting messages about boldness. I'm guessing you've already seen this in action: you've experienced and recognized the trend.

In situations where I'm asked to present, or to lead—especially in the professional world—I'm often expected to be authoritative. We all are.

Since childhood, we've been told that in order to lead, we must be dominant—a trait that may or may not be natural. We're told that we must stand up for ourselves, establish ourselves as credible, and hide our emotions. After all, if we're too emotional we won't look bold, we won't look strong.

I'm not saying it's best that we cry our way to the top, or that it's even possible to do such a thing, but, I am saying that we need to rethink situations where boldness is necessary (by looking at what God himself tells us), and then we must establish what that may mean for us, especially as both women *and* believers.

Boldness and dominance don't need to be synonymous. They should not be—even if that's a correlation we've built based on the messaging that we've been programmed with since childhood. Remember, we were all created and wired differently. While boldness is required of each of us; it won't always look the same.

Establishing Why We're Here

To figure out what situations the Scriptures earlier in this chapter are referring to when they direct us to be bold and what that boldness might look like in our lives, we must establish why we're here in the first place.

If we believe that we, as Christians, are here to follow God, to love others as the Bible commands us, and to spread the message of God's love for us, proclaiming it through all the world—in our every day lives, wherever it is God has placed us or will place us in the future—then we're off to a pretty good start.

If our purpose is to point others to our father in heaven,

then, it's logical to assume that this is where we should be bold. To gain this boldness, instead of looking inward, or outward to outside influencers, we must begin by looking up and, as we discussed in Chapter 8, surrendering our will to God, asking him for boldness to live out his calling and plans for our lives.

Maybe this is why Hebrews 4:16 tells us to, *with confidence* [boldness] *draw near to the throne of grace, that we may receive mercy and find grace to help in time of need.*

Our boldness comes from seeking out God's will for our lives, establishing ourselves firmly in him, practicing gratitude for whatever it is he would have for us and moving forward in truth with confidence.

If we lean back on ourselves, or evaluate where we—alone, just us—have fallen short in the boldness department, we're back to leaning on ourselves again: this is the cycle we must break, the one we find ourselves in so often.

What This Kind of Boldness Might Mean for You

Now, as we've established, some of us might be more assertive by nature. Some of us might be decision-makers who push limits and race full force ahead into whatever might be waiting. And, if that is how God has built you, *that's okay,* wonderful, even!

But, if this definition of boldness is what we strive for because it's what outside forces tell us we should be, *not* because it's how God has built us, then, we will fall short. Every. Single. Time.

What is boldness in your life? What might it look like?

- It might mean making parenting choices that look strange to those around you who accuse you of sheltering your kids, or being too free-range (it's always one extreme or the other, but "different" is generally the common denominator).
- It might mean *not* actively seeking to climb the corporate ladder.
- It might mean packing up your family and moving across the country or world to follow a call God has placed in your heart and confirmed through prayer and the encouragement of other believers.
- It might mean choosing a public school that's outside of the norm for other families in your church, choosing a private school that's outside the norm for families in your neighborhood, or homeschooling, depending on the needs of your kids and the unique challenges you face.
- It might mean breaking off a relationship that has caused nothing but hurt, or, has caused you to act in a manner outside of the standard God has set for your life.
- It might mean switching career paths altogether, without really knowing what's up ahead.
- It might mean befriending someone who others might not approve of, or—let's be honest ladies because this is real and it happens frequently, we may even be guilty of it ourselves if we want to be 100 percent honest—have shunned altogether.

I don't know your story, even though I wish I could sit down and have coffee with almost anyone while listening to their stories: I'm passionate about this. But, maybe one of the scenarios above hits home. Perhaps, though, it's something else altogether. None of us fits into a neat little package or pattern.

We. Are. Different!

To figure out what's next, we find a common foundation. It's this: the most important part of God's call for boldness and courage, is that we seek him first, establishing him as the center of our lives and that we live with gratitude each day for the blessings he has bestowed upon our lives, continually seeking his will, spending time in his word, and asking him to provide the guidance we need for moving forward.

Unfortunately, this is so opposite from what we hear from some of the loudest voices in our lives. Can women be world leaders who shape societies, rebuild companies, and create multi-million-dollar brands from the ground up?

Absolutely.

But, when these voices, voices with tens of thousands of followers who tell you how to model their success and use it as the basis for your own measure of success, become the only voices you hear and the only voices you follow, you're setting yourself up for failure.

Even if God's plan for your life *does* look the same as what they've achieved, your path forward probably looks different. Sure, it's great to learn from others. However, when we try to learn so much that we believe their path is automatically the best path, or, that their dreams should be our dreams, we're setting ourselves up for failure.

These women who've paved paths forward have done and achieved extraordinary things: there's no doubt about it. But, God's story for your life is so much more than just to follow someone else's lead. He has a plan for you and has given you your own dreams for a reason: be bold in this knowledge, no matter what that looks like.

Know that the emotions he has given you, the tendencies he has built you on, the relationships he has placed in your path, and the experiences he has built into your story are valuable; they're uniquely yours and every single one has a purpose, whether you can see it yet or not. Trusting in this foundation and believing this truth is what will set you up for your greatest successes—not a single blueprint that an influencer provides or a thousand leadership seminar lessons filled with flashy words meant to inspire you to chase the same dream as everyone else (how boring would this be?).

In this life—with a solid foundation of gratitude, prayer, and study—we can be bold, chasing the dreams that God has placed on our hearts with the skills he has individually blessed us with to accomplish those dreams.

While We're on the Topic of Dreams

It's important that we don't start to believe that following

God's plan means a boring, complacent life, or, that we begin to think that in dreaming, we are automatically focusing on our own lives.

Some of our dreams may be fleeting or completely beyond our grasp. My oldest son wants to be an NBA player. When we talk about the future, it always boils down to something like "Well, I guess I'll go to college but just to play basketball to prepare for the NBA. Then I'll make so much money I'll never need to work."

I will certainly not be the one to squash his hopes. At least not now when he's 10. However, he has yet to score a single basket in a basketball game and is one of the shortest boys in his grade. I want him to keep dreaming, and I want him to keep loving the game. But, at some point, I hope he starts to recognize his other skills—skills founded in the way God has shaped him: he's a born leader. He is competitive. He is gifted in math. Someday, my prayer is that God begins to use these other giftings to point Colin toward whatever it is God has for his life, and that his dreams begin to come into focus with that as the foundation. If it's the NBA? Awesome. I'll be in the stands at each and every game screaming my head off. If it's something more "ordinary" (or, "boring" as he would say), I'll still be cheering him on wholeheartedly while praying that God continues to direct his path.

Me? I wanted to be a country music star. Let's be clear: I have NEVER been awarded any sort of musical solo. While I did make select chorus as a child, the only plausible explanation starts and ends with my Mom being best friends with the music teacher. "Tone-deaf" might be a kind way of describing my vocal capabilities. My husband can account for this, and has laughed at my inability to judge my own vocal abilities on multiple occasions.

Now: I'm clearly never going to sing at the Grand Ole Opry. However, as I've grown, my love of music has too. It's how I best connect with God. It's often tied into how I remember certain points in my life. It's driven me to sit down at the piano when nothing else makes sense. Music is a part of my heart. While my original dream may have been a little—or a lot—far-fetched, I think God placed the foundation of it there to help me better connect with him.

The same goes for writing. Throughout my life, God has placed different leaders, teachers, and friends in my life who have verified that writing is how I communicate best. It has opened doors for conversations with friends—and strangers—that I didn't even know were struggling. It's helped me sort out challenging times in my own life because somehow, when I sit down with a pen, I'm better able to see God's truth about the way I'm feeling. It's also how—at hard points in our dating relationship and marriage I've communicated my feelings to my husband. I'll never be a famous poet or write fabulous fiction that draws people to another time and place (though I am so grateful for individuals God has blessed in this way!), but, just maybe I'll be better able to share whatever it is God has for my life if

I base my dreams on the ability he gave me to write things down.

This is true for all of us. We all have dreams. Some may seem crazy. Some might just be crazy. But, if we look back at our stories, the validation of others in our lives, and the times God has had the helm of our lives, and we base our dreams on what we find, we'll be off to a better start.

In these dreams? We should be bold. We should pursue them while praying constantly for God to direct our paths and open our eyes, while asking those closest to us to do the same. Boldness is a gift, however, if applied to the wrong circumstances, it will fall short, leaving us *feeling* small as a result at best, or, like complete failures at worst.

Our dreams are a part of who we are, and they might just help lead us to what God has for us. They may help us find areas in which we should be bold and they might lead us to bigger and better things than we could come up with on our own.

God's plan is so big and his love is so deep: guys, just think about that for awhile and give it all up to him. Then, go forward with confidence and chase down the dreams he's placed in your heart, constantly leaning on and listening to him. This is a boldness so different from what the world has to offer, but so much better!

It's a boldness rooted in reason, fueled by a hefty dose of gratitude. Imagine the possibilities!

Questions to Consider

1. How does starting with gratitude help us be more bold? What does the scripture tell us about being bold? Write down a few highlights from the Bible about boldness and confidence.

2. In what areas of life do you feel God prompting you to be more bold? What validation has he provided about this? Does it require more prayer? Who can you ask to pray for you in this specific area?

3. What dreams have you had since childhood? What gifts has God blessed you with that align with those dreams? What might he be prompting you to pursue?

4. What one step do you feel like God might be prompting you to take today toward the dreams he's placed on your heart?

10

Practical Application

Here we are.

The finish line is just up ahead, as we round the final corner. We are so close—this is exciting!

We've established the basis and importance of gratitude in our daily lives, and we've sorted through how biblical gratitude is different from the gratitude this world tells us to chase. We know that it's heart deep, more than just an action.

We've dug into our personal stories to identify how God has been writing and weaving them together from the beginning, and how, starting small, we can begin to use them to draw closer to God while encouraging others on their own journeys and in their own relationships with him.

We've begun to discuss how we can be bold in our daily

lives, and how we *can* dare to dream big by understanding why we're here in the first place.

Y'all . . . this is exciting. It's time to put it all together, making a plan for changing the way we view and steward what we've been handed and entrusted with. Each and every one of us is unique yet, we're tied together in this story that's so very much bigger than anything we could have ever imagined on our own.

So. Where do we start? How can we take simple steps to make intentional gratitude part of our daily lives, part of what we do naturally every step of every day?

We. Start. Small.

This is generally a good prerogative with any initiative in life. Giant steps often lead to giant setbacks when we don't quite measure up.

Instead, our small start begins with the scripture we've examined throughout this book, the examples of those who've gone before us, and what we know. We take action that leads us down a path that leads toward a heart-deep gratefulness that is transformative, drawing us closer to the Savior who's been drawing us toward himself from day one until today.

Below are a few practical steps for getting started and going deep. Some of them overlap a bit—that's okay. Sometimes that's what's necessary for us to allow real heart-deep change to take place.

Now's a great time to decide whether you're serious about this grateful living thing; if you are, commit fully and go all the way. I promise: it's worth it. But don't take my word for it. See for yourself.

Pray Prayers of Surrender: Mean Them

Time and time again I have had conversations with close friends and with women I've just met, where the theme of group work and projects has come up.

The conversations often go like this:

"I was working with so and so on [insert class project, work assignment, or even a home improvement task] and nothing was getting done." Or, "progress was so slow." Or, "I just couldn't wait for the team to figure it out."

The exact situation varies from one conversation to the next, but, the theme is the same: as women, we're often programmed to be efficient doers of various tasks. We're also often programmed to not be the best at waiting, especially when we see a better way of just pushing through to get a specific task done. Some of us obviously have more patience than others and some of us are better at giving out grace than others (by "some of us," I'm unfortunately not referring to myself), but a common thread is that at the end of the day, we are individuals who like to take control and get things done.

When it comes to our individual relationships with God, this can be problematic.

We're good at understanding the fact that he's in control

of all things and that he has a plan that will come together at some point in time to bring glory to himself while drawing people to his heart.

But, then we look at his plan for our lives in the same way we look at group projects, forgetting that this is not a group project at all: it's his divine plan that we get to be a part of. When we start to take charge, we indicate that we know better and that our way will be better, even when we know that isn't true at all.

Which brings us back to the idea of surrender. That song I mentioned earlier in the book? I need to start every single day with it as my prayer to God. I'm guessing you do too.

"Not my will today, God. But yours be done."

"Not my strength, God. But yours alone."

"I surrender."

Sing it if you need to. However you pray it, mean it.

By starting each day with a very serious, very intentional prayer of surrender—whether I enjoy not being in control or not—I'm giving him room to work in my heart, and to direct my path.

Some days it's harder than others. Sometimes that prayer hurts. Sometimes it goes against every part of my own personal desire. But, by making it the start of each day, I know that no matter what I walk through, I will be able to look at it as his will, and will be reminded that his purpose is better than mine.

I cannot live each day with a grateful heart unless he is

at the helm, directing each moment, each interaction, each conversation, and each situation that I may find myself in.

You can't either. We are all in this together.

It's easy to think we can be grateful without much heart change, but that puts us back on the path of shallow gratitude that allows us to feel in control and to choose the blessings we will acknowledge.

Surrender is an essential first step. Can you give God complete control of your whole life, not just parts of it? Can you truly surrender, even if it hurts?

Get in the Word

Any self-help guru or business leader will tell you the same thing: what you choose to dwell on is what you will become.

Even Oprah Winfrey herself has said it:

I know for sure that what we dwell on is who we become.[1]

It's why in this book we've spent a whole chapter talking about dwelling on the right thing (God's word) and using it a lamp that lights the path for every single encounter you have throughout each and every day.

If we want to live our lives with intentional gratitude— we've got to go to the source, we've got to start with scripture. Spending time reading words that are inspired by God and/or spoken by his son is just as important as

---

[1] Winfrey, Oprah. "Oprah's Words to Live By." *Oprah.com.* N.p. Web. 11 Nov. 2020.

surrendering our lives and our wills to him every day. We must dwell on the giver of every good and perfect thing if we want to truly appreciate what he's done in our hearts and in our lives.

We can't have it both ways: we cannot dwell on the voices that surround us on social media, in the news, and in our conversations with friends and co-workers and family, and measure our lives and our worth according to them . . . and also dwell on God's word and use it as the basis for every part of our day and the worth we feel as image bearers of him.

We must choose and we must act accordingly.

To live our lives with eternal, intentional gratitude to our Lord while transforming our minds and actions to impact our communities, our families, and those in our world, we must spend time reading the Bible, using the truth we find to inform our actions as we go about our lives.

When the Bible is the foundation you build upon and what you dwell on first, everything else—all the other voices and messages—will fall into the right place.

Start by committing to a chapter or two each day. I know we *know* that reading the Bible is important, but I shared my struggle with this earlier in the Bible . . . we've got to make it a priority.

Pick a reading plan that makes sense for your lifestyle, upload a Bible app on your phone, pick a devotional that points you back to scripture. Whatever you do, make it a regular part of each day. Over time, you'll find yourself craving more and more.

Give it a go: it's something you can't possibly regret.

Reflect on God's Goodness: Pray

As you surrender your heart to the Lord and get into his word, make sure you leave time to reflect, both in your own heart and in honest prayer and conversation with God.

Reflection is built into who we are. We're meant to think about certain things, and to use the information we have to relate to others and to be who we've been created to be. Reflecting on God's goodness in our lives, in the lives of people since the beginning of time, and in the world around us, even when "good" is hard to find, is absolutely critical for gratitude-filled living.

It requires quiet and stillness—which, we've acknowledged can be hard to find in today's world, but that doesn't make it unimportant. It requires taking a break from our 100 mph lifestyles. It requires taking a few deep breaths. Reflection doesn't work so well if we can't steady ourselves for a few minutes each day.

There's a reason the Bible tells us over and over again to "be still." It takes intention, it takes effort: we aren't hardwired for stillness!

It means we have to commit. (Ahem: once again, we need to get intentional).

This might look different for each of us. But, after we read the words of Scripture, we should take what we learn to the Lord, asking him to help us understand what we've read, while reflecting on his goodness through it all.

One of my favorite examples of the importance of prayer comes from well-known Christian speaker Louis Giglio. He says, "If we could see what happens when we pray, we would never cease to pray!"[2]

In his examples, God dispatches angels to various parts of the world, works in hearts and ACTS upon our prayers, whether we realize it or not.

To improve our prayer lives and to build gratitude within our hearts, we must think of prayer as a constant intercession with the Lord . . . not an act that we use to go through the motions of Christian life each day.

To take it one step further, Giglio tells us that we should be *"people who stand in the gap"* between the earthly world we live in, and the heavenly realm of our God.

Once again: this is a personal act that has giant ripple effects into how we handle every interaction, every day. God is good: reflecting on what we learn about his character, through his word, can help us better understand this. Taking our requests, our praises and our thoughts to our Lord in prayer is absolutely critical to living gratitude-filled lives.

Don't neglect this step!

---

[2] "20 Inches to Mercy (If My People Pray) - Louie Giglio." *YouTube*, Passion City Church, 23 Mar. 2020, www.youtube.com/watch?v=0fNFY76XNXc.

Write It Down

Journaling is good for, well . . . pretty much everyone.

Writing down our thoughts helps us channel our focus, helps us center in on how we're feeling, and actually improves health by lessening anxiety and stress.[3]

We think better when we write our thoughts down. Better yet: we focus most on the things we're able to put on paper.

See where I'm heading here?

What if we took what we know about journaling, and we bring it back to gratitude? (Note: I am NOT advocating that this replace all other forms of journaling. If you already write regularly, maybe consider adding it to your routine.)

The best part? It's super simple.

Start each day, after spending time in God's word and listening for him, surrendering yourself to his will and praying, by writing down the things you're grateful for.

Start small: think 3 things.

These could be *any* things: your family. A blessing you noticed recently. People to do laundry for. A situation at work. A flower blooming outside. A sunny day. Rain for your garden. A cute moment with your pet.

I don't know what you're grateful for today, or, what you'll be grateful for tomorrow, but, by intentionally listing out your thoughts, you'll be bringing gratitude to the

---

[3] "Journaling for Mental Health." *University of Rochester Medical Center.* N.p. Web. 11 Nov. 2020.

forefront of your mind, and using it to jumpstart each day.

As you go—it will get easier and easier, reshaping how you see the world around you. I can also promise you'll quickly grow out of limiting yourself to just three things.

The thing about this practice is that you need to keep it up, whether you want to or not.

Having a bad day? Receive terrible news? Moments like that might make it hard to be grateful, but, I'd argue that those are the times we need to think outside of our current emotions and cling to gratitude even more tightly, better aligning ourselves with our God and his "bigger" picture and plan for our lives.

Grab a journal and get going. It doesn't take long, and yet, it's so important. As time goes on, or, you find yourself struggling, flip back over the pages of past days. What you find might be exactly what you need to press on and move forward.

Think About Your List

If it seems like intentional gratitude requires a lot of intentional thought, that's because it does.

While we've already gone deep into the importance of dwelling on God's word and seeking his direction, this step is slightly different.

As you march through each day, think about the words you wrote down in the morning. What are you grateful for?

When you're frustrated by a situation at your child's

school . . . think about something you're grateful for that you wrote down in the morning.

When someone cuts you off in traffic when you're already late to an appointment and frustration is running high: think about your list.

When your team at work is struggling to meet a deadline and to understand one another's opinions: counter the anger that starts to boil up with gratitude.

Get the picture? Great.

As everyday events bring everyday frustrations: go back to the list. Think about something you're grateful for. Simple. Straightforward. Important.

Share: Talk About It

As you consider ways to focus on gratitude, changing the lens through which you view the world around you and the purpose God may have for you being a part of it, it's important to remember that the process might be a slow one.

For me, it all started with laundry . . . but, reframing the way I see the world and my Savior took several years; and to be honest, it's still a work in progress.

Having said that—this might seem like *a lot.* This is especially true when we start using words like "share" and "talk about it."

I'm an introvert. I find that I recharge in moments of quiet. To be perfectly honest, I'd be pretty content to stay at home with my family and a few good books for longer than I should probably admit.

But: that's not why I'm here.

God gave me the ability to connect with others. In addition, he's commanded me—and each of you—to love others and to share about him as we go about our daily lives: to our families, to our children, to our co-workers, to our neighborhoods, to our friends.

For some, this might mean committing to a life of international missions work.

For others, this might mean sharing our stories as we discussed earlier, and just pointing out things we're grateful for in everyday conversation.

It might mean opening up our homes and dining room tables to others, even when we are stressed or overwhelmed or tired or "done," and being honest about exactly where we are in that moment.

The thing is: people are used to complaints. We are surrounded by a negative news cycle. We're surrounded by messages that tell us we don't quite measure up. That we should work out more. That we should work harder to earn more. That we should value our time. That we should chase happiness with everything. Each of these examples screams the same: "*run for the future, keep moving forward, where you are right now isn't enough.*"

When we live in constant gratitude for the here and now, the *everyday* moments, we begin to realize that right now is an okay place to be.

Sure. There's always room to improve. But, appreciating the "right now" is a critical calling that we often miss.

That *doesn't* mean sharing a constant stream of #blessed posts.

Of course—sharing openly on social media can be a way to connect with others, especially during times that make in-person connections challenging. But, it could mean pointing out what you're grateful for, and giving credit to God—the one who gave you whatever that moment, thing, person, or place might be.

It *is* possible to be incredibly grateful out in the open, without bragging, or without having the motivation to position yourself above any other person. Being open, honest, and transparent is key. If you're going to share the good, share the real.

Which leads us to another important point . . .

Check Your Motivation

I'm talking to all of us on this one. Me too. Meeeee too.

We are built to make ourselves appear positive to those around us. There's something inside us that wants desperately to impress just about everyone, even if we don't consider people pleasing one of our core traits. Maybe it's because of the messages that have been impressed upon us since we were small:

- Those clothes are unflattering.
- Name brands matter: cars, clothes, you name it, the logo it carries has mattered since you could read (maybe even before).
- You need to build your resume to climb to the top.

- Your home search should include finding the "wow" factor.

If we aren't impressing those around us, somehow, we've adopted the mindset that we aren't enough.

So, we overcompensate. We post all the pictures with just the right angles in the best location. When we don't have anything great in the moment to share, we go with vacations and travel from the past, flashing back to the better moments. We track likes, we "love" the comments that help build us up, all while acting like none of it matters at all (even though we believe deep down that we need it). We search for validation everywhere.

When we find ourselves in this place, digging out can be an enormous challenge. This means we've got to stop it before it starts.

It's okay if today is where you start. Remember: living in the past solves nothing. We are looking forward here, sister. Full. Speed. Ahead.

Every single time you go to post something on social or share a story with an embellishment or two with a friend . . . pause. Ask yourself "Why?"

What is my motivation in sharing this post?
Is it pointing to me and my accomplishments?
Am I seeking compliments?

OR:

Is it going to point people to the creator of my life in a

clear and compelling way that starts conversations and
screams of God's grace in my life . . . in the good times
and the bad?

Look, we aren't going to get it right every time. We are
going to fall short. But, by checking our motivation before
we open our mouths or push "share," we might be able to
course-correct.

Keep Jesus' words in mind: *where your treasure is, there*
your heart will be also (Matthew 6:21).

Be Bold

In chapter 9, we discussed how gratitude is foundational
for boldness (and vice versa, the two go hand-in-hand), and
that God's boldness sometimes looks different than the
world's boldness.

When you've surrendered your heart, your actions, and
your motivations to God, and you've centered your heart
on gratitude for every moment, every thing, and every encounter, you can go forward with boldness: you are not
alone. You are not left to your own devices.

As you think about what the future might hold, the decisions you must make, and the way you live your
"everyday" or your "normal," and you're sure that you are
aligning your heart with God's plan for your future, you
can be bold.

You can replace timidness, uncertainty, and anxiety

with a calm assurance that you don't need to rely on yourself anymore.

This sort of boldness? This is the peace that passes understanding that we're promised in Philippians chapter 4. This is so important.

Be bold. You are loved by a love that has existed since before the world was formed and before you were a thought in anyone's mind: a love that's based on nothing in this world and will last forever.

Whew!

Be Generous

Psalm 112, verse 5, tells us that good will come to those who are generous and lend freely, who conduct their affairs with justice (NIV).

We've already talked a lot about how "good" doesn't always mean Earthly blessing, and how we may view what is good differently than God, but, this verse is clear: we are called to be generous *and* to seek justice.

We are called to be there—whatever "there" may look like—for those in need.

This could mean those in need of someone to listen and share burdens. Those in need of physical goods. Those in need of someone to stand firm in truth for them. Those in need of kindness.

While we may be called to be generous with our finances or earthly belongings—which I would argue we should be if God has blessed us this way—we should also be generous with our time.

Y'all. People who choose to live this way look different in the best possible way . . . more than any social media post, more than any humblebrag, more than almost anything else they could possibly do.

Our world is about getting ahead and staying on top, pursuing happiness and wealth. We know this. There's no arguing it and no avoiding it. So, when someone lives for others, truly putting themselves on the back burner for the good of those around them, it's, well . . . weird, especially to those who don't understand.

It leads to questions. Sometimes, it leads to conversations.

If I were to point to any one thing that has led to conversations about my beliefs with non-believers, it's that sometimes how my husband and I live our lives looks ridiculous to those around us.

I'm not kidding or exaggerating. The words we've heard tossed around among our non-believing friends commonly include "weird," "strange," "crazy," and "ridiculous."

These terms generally come across as positive (which sounds crazy, but they're generally not accompanied by negative connotations). I'm not sharing this to build us up. We mess up every single day. Most days more than once. But, in being transparent—even in the mistakes—we've had more meaningful conversations than any time we've decided on our own to set up and direct a conversation.

To make an impact in this world, and in the circles God has placed us in, sometimes we need to live differently.

I don't know if you've gotten to watch any of the series "The Chosen," or not, but it illustrates this point—from the source himself, Jesus Christ—really well.[4]

Co-written, directed, and created in 2017 by Dallas Jenkins, the series follows the relationships Jesus built with his followers, and his interactions with others during his ministry and life here on Earth. At publishing time, the first season and second seasons have aired and the conversations it has started are deep.

One of the show's taglines is "Get used to different."

Our Savior's life—the example we are to follow—was the kind of *different* that people noticed, the kind of different that placed others first, getting to the heart of the matter instead of making assumptions and judgments upfront. It was a life lived generously and it changed the world.

By living differently, starting with heart-deep gratitude that extends to outside generosity, we can help point others to that example.

Repeat. Repeat. Repeat.

Grateful living might take time to take hold. But, like any other habit, repetition is key.

Take the steps we just covered and listen to how God leads you. Continue to learn, continue to press forward,

---

[4] "The Chosen." *Watch.angelstudios.com*, Angel Studios, watch.angelstudios.com/thechosen/the-chosen.

continue to live with intentional gratitude. Then, wake up and do it again. And again. And again.

If we—as believers—band together, committing to walk in the steps of our Savior while lifting each other up and thanking him for the way he poured out his life for each of us, we might just be on to something. We might be able to reach those around us. We might just become the unified light this world craves.

Heart change is real . . . and it changes everything. Can you commit to living with intentional gratitude and watching what happens next?

Let's do this together. Let's go.

Lord. Change our hearts. Take hold of our lives, help us surrender to you, and see the blessings you've poured out on our lives, whether they resemble what we consider "traditional" blessings or not. Help us dig deep and cling to you along the way. Lord, transform us; allow us to be imitators of you. Allow us to live with grateful hearts.

Amen.

With Gratitude

No thanks can be shared without looking at the source of it all. I'm so grateful for the Lord, for his leading (sometimes gentle, sometimes less gentle) in my life, and for his no-matter-what love that's been on display through it all: the mountains, the valleys, the waiting, the going, and the everyday. My story is thanks to his intricate weaving and planning, as is yours.

One of the main players he made a part of this story and journey is my husband, John. John: thank you for allowing me to share our story with transparency—even the hard parts. Thank you for patience. Thank you for encouragement. Thank you for giving me space to reflect, and time to reflect. Thank you for loving our family well.

For my kids: your patience during Mommy's long hours

in front of a computer when you would have rather been crafting, baking, or running around: thank you. My heart will always belong to the five of you: Colin, Lucas, Andrew, Virginia, and Levi.

When the world went into lockdown with an uncertain future, loneliness was a natural consequence for so many. During this time, I (and my whole family) was gifted an extra special blessing: neighbors here, where we were planted. I'm so grateful for my neighbor ladies. From socially distanced outdoor fire pit nights, and garage football games to long walks where we talked about anything and everything, I was inspired, encouraged, and loved on. I'm not sure I can express how much you all lightened the load.

For those who took the time to listen to my concept for this book from day 1, approximately 5 years ago, to those who challenged ideas within it, read it, and shared critical feedback, thank you. While my name is on the cover, your thoughts and ideas sharpened the words inside, and made it what it is.

For influencers who continue to stay on the narrow path, pointing women just like me to the Lord in the everyday: you have inspired me, have provided encouragement without knowing it, and have shaped who it is I aspire to be. Continue in your missions: they are so impactful! You are on kingdom-growing missions with eternal results!

Bible Passages on Gratitude

Want to dive into more of what scriptures tell us about gratitude?

Wonderful!

Dive into a few of—or all—of the passages below to go deeper.

Note: This is in no way all-inclusive. That would be nearly impossible. God's word has so much to tell us on the topic.

Rather, consider these a starting point for going deeper, just the very tip of the iceberg. If getting into the word is something intimidating to you, consider checking out a daily Bible reading plan, to walk you through the process: so many amazing resources are available for free online!

I promise, spending more time in the word is something

you'll never regret.

Onward. Check out these passages relating to gratitude:

- Psalm 118
- Colossians 3:12–17
- Philippians 4
- 1 Chronicles 16:8–36
- 2 Corinthians 4:7–18
- Psalm 9
- James 1:17–18
- Psalm 107

Other Helpful Resources

Other than scripture itself—which again, guys, I cannot emphasize enough, *get in the word!!*—there's no other single authority here on Earth around which we can build our lives.

However, there are a ton of well-written books and studies that, if you're struggling to find clarity, need a boost of encouragement in your walk with the Lord, or, are just looking to learn, may be helpful for you. Some of these were referenced throughout the book, some were not.

I've included a few that you may find helpful below (some were referenced throughout the book):

- Jennie Allen: *Made for This: 40 Days to Living Your Purpose*
- Jamie Ivey: *You Be You*

- Candace Cameron Bure: *100 Days of Joy and Strength*
- Ruth Chou Simons: *Beholding and Becoming: The Art of Everyday Worship*
- Francis Chan: *Crazy Love*
- David Platt: *Radical*

About the Author

Laura Pyne is a follower of Jesus, wife, mom of five, blogger and digital marketing professional who believes in sharing stories that point readers back to what matters most: deepening their relationships with God in a world that screams otherwise. A firm believer in embracing life's imperfections and taking each moment as it comes, Laura encourages women to live this life by building each other up together and is passionate about finding joy in every journey.